MEDITERRANEA
COOKBOOK

2000+ Days of Yummy 5 Ingredients Recipes, Tailored for Two, Ready in 10 Minutes.

Meal Plan & Shopping List Included.

Olivia Davis

Table of Content

What is the Mediterranean Diet?

The Mediterranean Diet is a dietary pattern inspired by the traditional eating habits of populations living in the Mediterranean region, particularly in countries such as Greece, Italy, and Spain.

It is renowned for its numerous health benefits and has been extensively studied and promoted as a model for promoting overall well-being. Let's delve into the key components and principles that define the Mediterranean Diet:

KEY COMPONENTS:

1. Emphasis on Fresh and Local Produce:

- **Fruits and Vegetables:** A substantial portion of the diet is derived from a colorful array of fruits and vegetables, providing essential vitamins, minerals, and antioxidants.
- **Whole Grains:** Whole grains like barley, quinoa, and whole wheat are staples, offering complex carbohydrates and fiber.

2. Incorporating Healthy Fats:

- **Olive Oil:** The primary source of fat is extra virgin olive oil, known for its monounsaturated fats and rich antioxidant content.
- **Nuts and Seeds:** Almonds, walnuts, and sunflower seeds are commonly consumed, providing heart-healthy fats.

3. Lean Proteins: Seafood, Poultry, and Legumes:

- **Seafood:** Regular consumption of fish, particularly fatty fish like salmon and mackerel, contributes omega-3 fatty acids for heart health.
- **Poultry:** Lean poultry such as chicken and turkey are preferred over red meat.
- **Legumes:** Beans, lentils, and chickpeas are excellent sources of protein and fiber.

4. Whole Grains and Fiber-Rich Foods:

- **Whole Grains:** Incorporating whole grains such as brown rice, whole wheat bread, and bulgur provides sustained energy and dietary fiber.
- **Fiber-Rich Foods:** High-fiber foods like fruits, vegetables, and legumes promote digestive health and contribute to a feeling of fullness.

5. Herbs, Spices, and Flavorful Seasonings:

- Herbs and Spices: Mediterranean cuisine relies on the aromatic flavors of herbs and spices like basil, oregano, rosemary, and garlic, reducing the need for excessive salt.
- Citrus Fruits: Lemons and oranges add zest to dishes, enhancing flavor without relying on excessive salt or unhealthy condiments.

6. Moderate Consumption of Dairy and Red Wine:

- Dairy: Greek yogurt and cheese are consumed in moderation, providing calcium and probiotics.
- Red Wine: Moderate consumption of red wine, particularly during meals, is associated with heart health benefits due to its antioxidants.

NUTRITIONAL PRINCIPLES:

1. Balancing Macronutrients:

- **Healthy Balance:** The diet emphasizes a balance between carbohydrates, fats, and proteins, with an emphasis on healthy fats and complex carbohydrates.

2. Antioxidants and Polyphenols:

- **Abundance of Antioxidants:** Fruits, vegetables, olive oil, and nuts contribute to a high intake of antioxidants, protecting cells from oxidative stress.

3. Omega-3 Fatty Acids:

- **Fatty Fish:** Regular consumption of fatty fish provides omega-3 fatty acids, which support heart health and cognitive function.

4. Maintaining a Healthy Caloric Intake:

- **Portion Control:** While not a strict low-calorie diet, the Mediterranean Diet encourages mindful eating and portion control, focusing on quality over quantity.

BENEFITS:

1. Heart Health:

- **Reduced Cardiovascular Risk:** The diet has been associated with lower rates of heart disease, attributed to the consumption of heart-healthy fats and antioxidants.

2. Weight Management:

- **Sustainable Weight Loss:** The emphasis on nutrient-dense foods and portion control supports weight management and sustainable weight loss.

3. Diabetes Management:

- **Blood Sugar Control:** The Mediterranean Diet has shown benefits in managing blood sugar levels, making it suitable for individuals with diabetes.

4. Longevity and Overall Well-Being:

- **Rich in Nutrients:** The diverse array of nutrient-dense foods contributes to overall health and longevity, with a focus on preventing chronic diseases.

CULINARY TRADITIONS AND LIFESTYLE:

1. Flavors of the Mediterranean:

Celebration of Flavor: The Mediterranean Diet embraces the joy of cooking and savoring the rich flavors derived from fresh, high-quality ingredients.

2. Cooking Methods and Culinary Traditions:

Simple Preparation: Meals are often prepared using simple cooking methods like grilling, roasting, and sautéing, preserving the natural flavors of the ingredients.

3. Regional Variations and Influences:

Diverse Cuisine: The Mediterranean region boasts diverse culinary traditions, with each country and region contributing its unique flavors and influences to the overall diet.

In essence, the Mediterranean Diet is not just a set of dietary guidelines; it's a holistic approach to life that prioritizes fresh, whole foods, mindful-eating, and a convivial atmosphere. Adopting the Mediterranean lifestyle can contribute to improved health, longevity, and a profound appreciation for the pleasures of good food.

Nutritional Principles

The nutritional principles of the Mediterranean Diet are rooted in a holistic approach to health, emphasizing nutrient-dense foods, balanced macronutrients, and a focus on overall well-being. Let's explore these principles in detail:

1. Balancing Macronutrients:

- **Healthy Balance:** The Mediterranean Diet emphasizes a well-balanced distribution of macronutrients – carbohydrates, fats, and proteins. While the exact proportions may vary, the emphasis is on maintaining a diet that is not overly skewed toward any one macronutrient.
- **Healthy Fats:** Monounsaturated fats, found abundantly in olive oil, nuts, and seeds, are a hallmark of the diet. These fats contribute to heart health and provide a satisfying source of energy.

2. Antioxidants and Polyphenols:

- **Abundance of Antioxidants:** The diet is rich in fruits, vegetables, nuts, and olive oil, all of which provide a diverse array of antioxidants. Antioxidants play a crucial role in neutralizing free radicals, protecting cells from damage, and supporting overall health.
- **Polyphenol-Rich Foods:** Herbs, spices, and certain beverages like red wine are sources of polyphenols, contributing to the diet's anti-inflammatory and disease-fighting properties.

3. Omega-3 Fatty Acids:

- **Fatty Fish:** The inclusion of fatty fish, such as salmon and mackerel, provides a significant source of omega-3 fatty acids. These essential fats are associated with heart health, cognitive function, and anti-inflammatory benefits.

- **Flaxseeds and Walnuts:** For those who may not consume fish regularly, sources like flaxseeds and walnuts also contribute omega-3 fatty acids.

4. Maintaining a Healthy Caloric Intake:

- **Portion Control:** While not strictly a low-calorie diet, the Mediterranean Diet encourages mindful eating and portion control. The focus is on savoring the quality of foods rather than consuming large quantities.
- **Nutrient Density:** The diet prioritizes nutrient-dense foods, ensuring that each calorie consumed provides a wealth of essential vitamins, minerals, and other beneficial compounds.

5. Whole Foods and Fiber:

- **Whole Grains:** Whole grains, such as brown rice, quinoa, and whole wheat, are integral to the diet, providing complex carbohydrates and fiber.
- **Fiber-Rich Foods:** Fruits, vegetables, legumes, and nuts contribute to the diet's high fiber content. Fiber supports digestive health, helps maintain a feeling of fullness, and may contribute to weight management.

6. Lean Proteins:

- **Fish and Poultry:** Fish, especially fatty fish like salmon, is a primary source of protein. Poultry, such as chicken and turkey, is preferred over red meat.
- **Legumes:** Beans, lentils, and chickpeas are excellent plant-based sources of protein, contributing to a balanced and diverse protein intake.

7. Moderate Consumption of Dairy and Red Wine:

- **Dairy:** Greek yogurt and cheese are consumed in moderation, providing calcium, probiotics, and additional protein.
- **Red Wine:** Moderate consumption of red wine, particularly during meals, is associated with heart health benefits due to its antioxidant content. However, moderation is key, and excessive alcohol consumption is discouraged.

PRACTICAL TIPS FOR ADHERING TO NUTRITIONAL PRINCIPLES:

1. Use Olive Oil as the Primary Cooking Fat:

- **Cooking and Drizzling:** Incorporate extra virgin olive oil into cooking and as a finishing touch to salads. Its monounsaturated fats contribute to heart health.

2. Prioritize Plant-Based Foods:

- **Vegetables and Fruits:** Aim to fill your plate with a variety of colorful vegetables and fruits. These foods provide essential vitamins, minerals, and antioxidants.

3. Include Fatty Fish Regularly:

- **Omega-3 Rich Choices:** Incorporate fatty fish, such as salmon, at least twice a week to ensure an adequate intake of omega-3 fatty acids.

4. Choose Whole Grains:

- **Diverse Grains:** Opt for whole grains like quinoa, brown rice, and whole wheat to provide sustained energy and fiber.

5. Enjoy Nuts and Seeds:

- **Handful of Goodness:** Include a handful of nuts and seeds, such as almonds and flaxseeds, as a snack or added to dishes for extra nutrients.

6. Explore Lean Protein Sources:

- **Fish, Poultry, Legumes:** Diversify your protein sources with fish, poultry, and legumes to ensure a well-rounded intake of amino acids.

7. Practice Portion Control:

- **Mindful Eating:** Be conscious of portion sizes and listen to your body's hunger and fullness cues. Avoid overeating and savor each bite.

8. Incorporate Herbs and Spices:

- **Flavorful Alternatives:** Use herbs and spices generously to add flavor to dishes, reducing the need for excessive salt or unhealthy condiments.

In summary, the nutritional principles of the Mediterranean Diet emphasize a balanced and diverse intake of nutrient-dense foods, showcasing the benefits of whole, fresh, and minimally processed ingredients. By adopting these principles, individuals can enjoy not only a delicious and varied diet but also the potential for improved health and well-being.

Benefits for Heart Health

The Mediterranean Diet has gained widespread recognition for its significant benefits in promoting heart health. Its association with lower rates of cardiovascular diseases and favorable impacts on various cardiovascular risk factors make it a recommended dietary pattern for individuals aiming to maintain a healthy heart.

Let's explore the detailed benefits for heart health provided by the Mediterranean Diet:

1. Impact on Cardiovascular Diseases:

- **Reduced Risk:** Numerous studies have consistently shown that adhering to the Mediterranean Diet is associated with a reduced risk of developing cardiovascular diseases, including coronary heart disease and stroke.
- **Lower Incidence of Heart Attacks:** The consumption of heart-healthy fats, antioxidants, and anti-inflammatory foods in the Mediterranean Diet contributes to a lower incidence of heart attacks.

2. Lowering Cholesterol Levels:

- **Monounsaturated Fats:** Olive oil, a key component of the Mediterranean Diet, is rich in monounsaturated fats. These fats have been shown to lower LDL (low-density lipoprotein) cholesterol levels, often referred to as "bad" cholesterol.
- **Omega-3 Fatty Acids:** Fatty fish, another staple in the diet, provides omega-3 fatty acids that help reduce triglyceride levels and increase HDL (high-density lipoprotein) cholesterol, known as "good" cholesterol.

3. Managing Blood Pressure:

- **Rich in Potassium:** The diet is naturally high in potassium, derived from fruits, vegetables,

and legumes. Potassium helps regulate blood pressure by balancing the effects of sodium.
- **Reduced Sodium Intake:** The Mediterranean Diet encourages the use of herbs and spices for flavoring, reducing the reliance on high-sodium condiments and processed foods.

4. Antioxidant Protection:

- **Abundance of Antioxidants:** Fruits, vegetables, nuts, and olive oil in the Mediterranean Diet are rich in antioxidants, such as polyphenols and vitamin C. These compounds protect cells from oxidative stress and inflammation.
- **Reduced Inflammation:** Chronic inflammation is a key contributor to cardiovascular diseases. The anti-inflammatory properties of foods in the Mediterranean Diet contribute to overall heart health.

5. Heart-Healthy Fats:

- **Olive Oil:** The monounsaturated fats in olive oil have been shown to improve the lipid profile, reducing the risk of atherosclerosis (hardening of the arteries) and coronary heart disease.
- **Nuts and Seeds:** Almonds and walnuts, commonly consumed in the diet, provide a mix of healthy fats, including omega-3 fatty acids.

6. Regulating Blood Sugar Levels:

- **Whole Grains:** The inclusion of whole grains, such as brown rice and whole wheat, supports stable blood sugar levels, reducing the risk of diabetes, a significant risk factor for heart disease.
- **High Fiber Content:** Fiber-rich foods, including fruits, vegetables, and legumes, contribute to improved glycemic control and insulin sensitivity.

7. Overall Cardiovascular Risk Reduction:

- **Combination of Factors:** It's important to note that the benefits for heart health in the Mediterranean Diet stem from the synergistic effects of various components. The combination of healthy fats, antioxidants, and nutrient-dense foods contributes to an overall reduction in cardiovascular risk.

8. Long-Term Maintenance of Cardiovascular Health:

- **Sustainable Lifestyle:** Unlike fad diets, the Mediterranean Diet is sustainable and can be adopted as a long-term lifestyle. Long-term adherence is crucial for maintaining cardiovascular health over the years.

9. Improving Endothelial Function:

- **Enhanced Blood Vessel Health:** The diet has been associated with improved endothelial function, which refers to the health of the blood vessels' inner lining. This contributes to better blood flow and reduced risk of clot formation.

In conclusion, the Mediterranean Diet stands out as a heart-healthy dietary pattern due to its diverse array of nutrient-dense foods, emphasis on healthy fats, and protective effects against cardiovascular risk factors.

By adopting the principles of the Mediterranean Diet, individuals can not only enjoy delicious and varied meals but also proactively support their heart health over the long term.

The Mediterranean Diet Pyramid

The Mediterranean Diet Pyramid is a visual representation of the traditional dietary pattern followed by people in the Mediterranean region. It offers a structured guide to the types and proportions of foods that form the foundation of this heart-healthy diet. Let's explore the key components of the Mediterranean Diet Pyramid in detail:

1. Foundation:

FRUITS, VEGETABLES, WHOLE GRAINS, AND LEGUMES:

- The base of the pyramid emphasizes the consumption of a variety of colorful fruits and vegetables, whole grains (such as whole wheat, barley, and oats), and legumes (beans, lentils, and chickpeas).
- These plant-based foods provide essential vitamins, minerals, fiber, and antioxidants.

2. Core:

OLIVE OIL:

- At the core of the Mediterranean Diet is the abundant use of extra virgin olive oil. It is the primary source of fat and is rich in monounsaturated fats and antioxidants.
- Olive oil is used for cooking, dressing salads, and as a condiment.

NUTS, SEEDS, AND WHOLE GRAINS:

- Nuts and seeds, including almonds, walnuts, and sunflower seeds, contribute healthy fats, protein, and essential nutrients.
- Whole grains, such as whole wheat bread, brown rice, and quinoa, offer complex carbohydrates and additional fiber.

FISH AND SEAFOOD:

- Fish and seafood, especially fatty fish like salmon and sardines, are recommended at least twice a week. They provide omega-3 fatty acids, promoting heart health.

3. Moderation:

POULTRY, EGGS, DAIRY, AND WINE:

- Poultry, eggs, and dairy products, including yogurt and cheese, are included in moderation.
- Red wine is consumed in moderation, particularly during meals. It is associated with cardiovascular health benefits due to its polyphenol content.

LEAN PROTEINS:

- Lean proteins such as poultry and eggs are chosen over red meat. These protein sources are consumed in moderate amounts to support muscle health.

4. Occasional:

RED MEAT:

- Red meat, including beef and pork, is considered an occasional indulgence rather than a daily staple. When consumed, it is in small portions.

SWEETS AND DESSERTS:

- Sweets and desserts, often featuring natural sweeteners like honey, are included sparingly. They are not a central part of daily meals but enjoyed occasionally.

5. Physical Activity and Social Connections:

PHYSICAL ACTIVITY:

- The Mediterranean Diet Pyramid extends beyond food to highlight the importance of regular physical activity. Exercise is integrated into the daily routine, promoting overall well-being.

SOCIAL CONNECTIONS:

- The pyramid emphasizes the social aspect of meals, encouraging communal dining and shared experiences. Gathering with family and friends around the table is a vital component of the Mediterranean lifestyle.

6. Enjoy Meals Mindfully:

SAVORING MEALS:

- Mindful eating is emphasized, encouraging individuals to savor and appreciate the flavors, textures, and aromas of each meal.
- Taking time to enjoy meals contributes to a more satisfying and balanced eating experience.

7. Hydration:

WATER AND HERBAL TEAS:

- Staying hydrated is essential. Water and herbal teas are recommended as the primary beverages.

8. Lifestyle Factors:

HEALTHY LIFESTYLE HABITS:

- The Mediterranean Diet Pyramid underscores the importance of lifestyle factors beyond food, including stress management, sufficient sleep, and a connection to nature.

9. Adaptation to Local and Seasonal Foods:

LOCAL AND SEASONAL EATING:

- The pyramid promotes the consumption of locally sourced and seasonal foods, emphasizing a connection to the environment and supporting sustainable practices.

10. Culinary Enjoyment:

CULINARY PLEASURE:

- Enjoying the process of cooking and relishing the sensory experience of meals is highlighted. The Mediterranean Diet places a premium on the joy of eating.

In summary, the Mediterranean Diet Pyramid is a holistic guide that extends beyond mere dietary recommendations. It encapsulates the principles of a balanced and enjoyable lifestyle that incorporates nutritious foods, regular physical activity, social connections, and mindfulness in eating habits.

Adopting this pyramid can contribute to overall health and well-being, emphasizing the enjoyment of food and life.

Myth Busters

While the Mediterranean Diet is widely recognized for its health benefits, there are several common myths and misconceptions associated with it. Clarifying these misunderstandings can help individuals better understand and adopt this dietary pattern effectively.
Let's explore these myths in detail:

1. Myth: All Fats are Bad, and the Mediterranean Diet is High in Fat.

- **Reality:** The Mediterranean Diet does include fats but primarily healthy fats. Extra virgin olive oil, a key component, is rich in monounsaturated fats, which are heart-healthy. Nuts and fatty fish also provide essential omega-3 fatty acids. The emphasis is on the quality of fats rather than their elimination.

2. Myth: It's Only About Olive Oil.

- **Reality:** While olive oil is a cornerstone of the diet, the Mediterranean Diet is not solely centered around it. It includes a diverse range of foods, such as fruits, vegetables, whole grains, nuts, seeds, legumes, fish, and lean proteins. The diet's effectiveness comes from the synergy of various nutrient-dense components.

3. Myth: Wine is Mandatory.

- **Reality:** While moderate consumption of red wine is a part of the Mediterranean lifestyle, it is not obligatory. If individuals do not consume alcohol or prefer alternatives, they can still follow the diet successfully by focusing on other aspects, such as a variety of plant-based foods and healthy fats.

4. Myth: Pasta and Bread Should Be Avoided.

- **Reality:** Whole grains, including whole grain pasta and bread, are integral to the Mediterranean Diet. However, portions are moderate, and emphasis is placed on choosing whole, minimally processed grains for their fiber content and nutritional benefits.

5. Myth: It's Expensive and Complicated.

- **Reality:** The Mediterranean Diet celebrates simple, fresh ingredients and does not require expensive or hard-to-find items. Seasonal and locally sourced produce, grains, and legumes form the basis of many dishes, making it accessible to a wide range of budgets.

6. Myth: It's Strict and Requires Counting Calories.

- **Reality:** The Mediterranean Diet is more about overall food patterns and lifestyle than strict calorie counting. It encourages mindful eating, portion control, and a focus on nutrient-dense foods rather than rigid rules.

7. Myth: Only Fish is Consumed for Protein.

- **Reality:** While fish is a prominent protein source, the diet also includes other lean proteins like poultry, legumes, nuts, and seeds. The emphasis is on a varied intake of protein sources for a well-rounded nutrient profile.

8. Myth: It's Only for Mediterranean Residents.

- **Reality:** The diet's name may suggest a regional limitation, but its principles can be adapted globally. The Mediterranean Diet's success lies in its emphasis on whole, unprocessed foods and a balanced lifestyle, making it suitable for people worldwide.

9. Myth: It's a Short-Term Solution for Weight Loss.

- **Reality:** The Mediterranean Diet is not a quick-fix solution. It's a sustainable, long-term lifestyle that promotes overall health. While weight loss may occur, the primary focus is on improving well-being and reducing the risk of chronic diseases.

10. Myth: Any Mediterranean Dish is Healthy.

- **Reality:** While many traditional Mediterranean dishes are healthy, some can be high in calories or contain excessive amounts of certain ingredients. Portion control and mindful choices are essential to ensure a balanced intake.

11. Myth: It's Only About Food.

- **Reality:** The Mediterranean Diet is not just a dietary pattern; it's a holistic lifestyle. Factors such as regular physical activity, social connections, and a positive approach to life contribute to its overall effectiveness.

12. Myth: It's One-Size-Fits-All.

- **Reality:** The Mediterranean Diet is adaptable. It can be personalized based on individual preferences, dietary restrictions, and cultural differences while still adhering to its core principles of whole, nutrient-dense foods.

In conclusion, dispelling these myths helps individuals approach the Mediterranean Diet with a more accurate understanding of its principles and benefits. It's a flexible and inclusive lifestyle that focuses on the overall well-being of individuals rather than imposing strict rules.

Breakfast

1. Greek Yogurt Parfait

Preparation time: 5 minutes
Servings: 2

Ingredients:

- 1 cup Greek yogurt
- 1 cup fresh mixed berries (strawberries, blueberries, raspberries)
- 2 tablespoons honey
- 2 tablespoons granola

Instructions:

1. In two serving glasses or bowls, layer 1/4 cup of Greek yogurt at the bottom.
2. Add a layer of mixed berries on top of the yogurt.
3. Drizzle 1 tablespoon of honey over the berries.
4. Repeat the layers with the remaining yogurt, berries, and honey.
5. Sprinkle 1 tablespoon of granola on each parfait as the final layer.
6. Serve immediately and enjoy your refreshing Greek Yogurt Parfait!

Nutritional Information (per serving):
Cal: 220 | Carbs: 34g | Pro: 12g | Fat: 5g
Sugars: 26g | Fiber: 4g

2. Mediterranean Veggie Omelette

Preparation time: 10 minutes
Servings: 2

Ingredients:

- 4 large eggs
- 1/2 cup diced tomatoes
- 1/2 cup chopped spinach
- 1/4 cup crumbled feta cheese
- Salt and pepper to taste

Instructions:

1. Crack the eggs into a bowl, beat them, and season with salt and pepper.
2. Heat a non-stick skillet over medium heat.
3. Pour the beaten eggs into the skillet, ensuring an even spread.
4. Scatter tomatoes and spinach over one-half of the eggs.
5. Sprinkle feta cheese on top.

6. Allow the omelette to cook until the edges start to set, then fold it in half.
7. Cook for an additional 1-2 minutes until the cheese melts.
8. Slide the omelette onto a plate, cut in half, and serve.

Nutritional Information (per serving):
Cal: 210 | Carbs: 5g | Pro: 17g | Fat: 14g
Sugars: 2g | Fiber: 2g

3. Whole Grain Toast

Preparation time: 5 minutes
Servings: 2

Ingredients:

- 4 slices whole grain bread, toasted
- 1/2 cup hummus
- 1 large tomato, thinly sliced
- Salt and pepper to taste

Instructions:

1. Toast the whole grain bread slices to your desired level of doneness.
2. Spread a generous layer of hummus on each slice.
3. Place the thinly sliced tomatoes on top of the hummus.
4. Sprinkle with salt and pepper to taste.
5. Serve immediately and enjoy this quick and nutritious breakfast!

Nutritional Information (per serving):
Cal: 280 | Carbs: 39g | Pro: 12g | Fat: 9g
Sugars: 5g | Fiber: 8g

4. Shakshuka (Poached Eggs in Tomato Sauce)

Preparation time: 10 minutes
Servings: 2

Ingredients:

- 4 large eggs
- 1 can (14 oz) crushed tomatoes
- 1 small onion, diced
- 2 cloves garlic, minced
- 1 teaspoon ground cumin
- Salt and pepper to taste

Instructions:

1. In a skillet, sauté the diced onion and minced garlic until softened.
2. Add the crushed tomatoes, ground cumin, salt, and pepper. Simmer for 5 minutes.
3. Make wells in the tomato sauce and crack eggs into them.
4. Cover the skillet and poach the eggs for 5 minutes or until the whites are set.
5. Spoon the sauce and eggs onto plates, ensuring each serving has two eggs.
6. Serve immediately with your favorite bread.

Nutritional Information (per serving):
Cal: 220 | Carbs: 18g | Pro: 14g | Fat: 10g
Sugars: 9g | Fiber: 5g

5. Feta and Spinach Breakfast Wrap

Preparation time: 10 minutes
Servings: 2

Ingredients:

- 4 large eggs, scrambled
- 1 cup fresh spinach leaves
- 1/2 cup crumbled feta cheese
- 2 whole wheat wraps
- Salt and pepper to taste

Instructions:

1. Scramble the eggs in a pan over medium heat until cooked.
2. In another pan, wilt the spinach leaves.
3. Warm the whole wheat wraps in a dry skillet or microwave.
4. Divide the scrambled eggs and spinach between the wraps.
5. Sprinkle each wrap with half of the crumbled feta cheese.
6. Season with salt and pepper to taste.
7. Fold in the sides and roll up the wraps.
8. Serve immediately for a delicious and satisfying breakfast.

Nutritional Information (per serving):
Cal: 380 | Carbs: 26g | Pro: 23g | Fat: 20g
Sugars: 2g | Fiber: 6g

6. Olive and Tomato Focaccia

Preparation time: 10 minutes
Servings: 2

Ingredients:

- 2 pieces of store-bought or homemade focaccia bread
- 1/2 cup Kalamata olives, pitted and sliced
- 1 cup cherry tomatoes, halved
- 2 tablespoons extra-virgin olive oil
- Fresh basil leaves for garnish

Instructions:

1. Preheat the oven to 350°F (180°C).
2. Place the focaccia bread on a baking sheet.
3. Scatter the sliced olives and halved cherry tomatoes evenly over the bread.
4. Drizzle extra-virgin olive oil over the top.
5. Bake in the preheated oven for 5-7 minutes or until the bread is warm.
6. Garnish with fresh basil leaves.
7. Slice and serve immediately as a delightful Mediterranean breakfast.

Nutritional Information (per serving):
Cal: 380 | Carbs: 46g | Pro: 8g | Fat: 19g
Sugars: 3g | Fiber: 3g

7. Quinoa Breakfast Bowl

Preparation time: 10 minutes
Servings: 2

Ingredients:

- 1 cup cooked quinoa
- 1 cup cherry tomatoes, halved
- 1 cup zucchini, sliced
- 2 tablespoons olive oil
- Salt and pepper to taste

Instructions:

1. Preheat the oven to 400°F (200°C).
2. Toss the halved cherry tomatoes and sliced zucchini in olive oil, salt, and pepper.
3. Roast the vegetables on a baking sheet for 8-10 minutes.
4. Divide the cooked quinoa between two bowls.
5. Top the quinoa with the roasted vegetables.
6. Drizzle with additional olive oil if desired.
7. Serve immediately for a nutritious and quick Mediterranean breakfast.

Nutritional Information (per serving):
Cal: 320 | Carbs: 36g | Pro: 7g | Fat: 18g

Sugars: 4g | Fiber: 6g

8. Orange and Almond Breakfast

Preparation time: 10 minutes
Servings: 2

Ingredients:

- 1 cup couscous, cooked
- 1 orange, peeled and segmented
- 1/4 cup almonds, sliced
- 2 tablespoons honey
- 1/2 teaspoon ground cinnamon

Instructions:

1. Cook the couscous according to package instructions.
2. Fluff the couscous with a fork and divide it between two bowls.
3. Top each bowl with orange segments and sliced almonds.
4. Drizzle 1 tablespoon of honey over each bowl.
5. Sprinkle ground cinnamon on top.
6. Stir gently and enjoy your vibrant and flavorful breakfast couscous.

Nutritional Information (per serving):
Cal: 320 | Carbs: 65g | Pro: 9g | Fat: 5g
Sugars: 20g | Fiber: 5g

9. Fig and Walnut Overnight Oats

Preparation time: 10 minutes (plus overnight soaking)
Servings: 2

Ingredients:

- 1 cup old-fashioned rolled oats
- 1 cup milk (dairy or plant-based)
- 4 dried figs, chopped
- 1/4 cup walnuts, chopped
- 2 tablespoons honey

Instructions:

1. In a bowl or jar, combine the rolled oats and milk.
2. Add chopped dried figs and walnuts to the mixture.
3. Stir well, cover, and refrigerate overnight.

4. In the morning, give the oats a good stir.
5. Divide the overnight oats into two bowls.
6. Drizzle 1 tablespoon of honey over each serving.
7. Enjoy your delicious and nutritious Fig and Walnut Overnight Oats.

Nutritional Information (per serving):
Cal: 420 | Carbs: 64g | Pro: 11g | Fat: 15g
Sugars: 28g | Fiber: 8g

10. Mediterranean Scrambled Tofu

Preparation time: 10 minutes
Servings: 2

Ingredients:

- 1 block (14 oz) firm tofu, crumbled
- 1/4 cup sun-dried tomatoes, chopped
- 2 tablespoons olive oil
- 1 teaspoon dried oregano
- Salt and pepper to taste

Instructions:

1. Heat olive oil in a skillet over medium heat.
2. Add crumbled tofu to the skillet, cooking for 3-5 minutes.
3. Stir in sun-dried tomatoes, dried oregano, salt, and pepper.
4. Cook for an additional 3-5 minutes until tofu is lightly browned.
5. Divide the scrambled tofu onto two plates.
6. Garnish with fresh herbs if desired.
7. Serve immediately and savor the flavors of Mediterranean Scrambled Tofu.

Nutritional Information (per serving):
Cal: 310 | Carbs: 9g | Pro: 20g | Fat: 22g
Sugars: 2g | Fiber: 3g

11. Greek-Style Pancakes

Preparation time: 5 minutes
Servings: 2

Ingredients:

- 1 cup pancake mix
- 3/4 cup water
- 1/2 cup Greek yogurt
- 2 tablespoons honey
- Fresh berries for topping

Instructions:

1. In a bowl, combine the pancake mix and water. Mix until just combined.
2. Heat a non-stick pan over medium heat.
3. Pour 1/4 cup of the pancake batter onto the pan for each pancake.
4. Cook until bubbles form on the surface, then flip and cook the other side until golden brown.
5. In a separate bowl, mix Greek yogurt and honey.
6. Serve the pancakes with a dollop of the yogurt-honey mixture & fresh berries on top.

Nutritional Information (per serving):
Cal: 350 | Carbs: 65g | Pro: 10g | Fat: 5g
Sugars: 25g | Fiber: 3g

12. Caprese Breakfast Sandwich

Preparation time: 10 minutes
Servings: 2

Ingredients:

- 2 whole grain English muffins, toasted
- 1 large tomato, sliced
- 4 slices fresh mozzarella cheese
- Fresh basil leaves
- Balsamic glaze for drizzling

Instructions:

1. Toast the whole grain English muffins.
2. On each muffin half, layer sliced tomato, fresh mozzarella, and basil leaves.
3. Drizzle with balsamic glaze.
4. Assemble into sandwiches and serve immediately.

Nutritional Information (per serving):
Cal: 320 | Carbs: 35g | Pro: 15g | Fat: 14g
Sugars: 5g | Fiber: 5g

13. Avocado and Chickpea Toast

Preparation time: 10 minutes
Servings: 2

Ingredients:

- 2 slices whole grain bread, toasted
- 1 ripe avocado, mashed

- 1/2 cup canned chickpeas, drained and rinsed
- Salt and pepper to taste
- Red pepper flakes for garnish (optional)

Instructions:

1. Toast the whole grain bread slices.
2. Spread mashed avocado evenly on each slice.
3. Top with chickpeas, and season with salt and pepper.
4. Optionally, garnish with red pepper flakes for a bit of heat.
5. Serve immediately.

Nutritional Information (per serving):
Cal: 280 | Carbs: 34g | Pro: 9g | Fat: 13g
Sugars: 1g | Fiber: 10g

14. Mediterranean Frittata

Preparation time: 10 minutes
Servings: 2

Ingredients:

- 4 large eggs
- 1/4 cup crumbled feta cheese
- 1/4 cup sliced Kalamata olives
- Salt and pepper to taste
- Fresh parsley for garnish

Instructions:

1. Preheat the broiler in your oven.
2. In a bowl, beat the eggs and season with salt and pepper.
3. Pour the beaten eggs into a non-stick, oven-safe skillet over medium heat.
4. Sprinkle feta and olives evenly over the eggs.
5. Cook on the stovetop until the edges begin to set.
6. Transfer the skillet under the broiler and cook until the top is set and slightly golden.
7. Garnish with fresh parsley and serve.

Nutritional Information (per serving):
Cal: 220 | Carbs: 3g | Pro: 14g | Fat: 17g
Sugars: 1g | Fiber: 1g

15. Chia Seed Pudding with Fresh Fruit

Preparation time: 5 minutes (plus overnight

chilling)
Servings: 2

Ingredients:

- 1/4 cup chia seeds
- 1 cup almond milk
- 1 tablespoon honey
- 1/2 teaspoon vanilla extract
- Fresh mixed berries for topping

Instructions:

1. In a jar, mix chia seeds, almond milk, honey, and vanilla extract.
2. Stir well, ensuring chia seeds are fully submerged.
3. Refrigerate overnight or for at least 4 hours until it thickens.
4. Stir well before serving, and top with fresh berries.

Nutritional Information (per serving):
Cal: 180 | Carbs: 22g | Pro: 4g | Fat: 9g
Sugars: 10g | Fiber: 10g

16. Spanakopita Muffins

Preparation time: 10 minutes
Servings: 2

Ingredients:

- 2 cups fresh spinach, chopped
- 1/2 cup crumbled feta cheese
- 2 large eggs
- 1/4 cup milk
- Salt and pepper to taste

Instructions:

1. Preheat the oven to 375°F (190°C) and grease two muffin cups.
2. In a bowl, combine chopped spinach and feta.
3. In a separate bowl, whisk eggs, milk, salt, and pepper.
4. Pour the egg mixture over the spinach and feta, and mix well.
5. Divide the mixture evenly into the muffin cups.
6. Bake for about 20 minutes or until set and slightly golden.
7. Allow to cool for a few minutes before serving.

Nutritional Information (per serving):
Cal: 220 | Carbs: 6g | Pro: 15g | Fat: 15g
Sugars: 2g | Fiber: 3g

17. Almond and Date Smoothie Bowl

Preparation time: 10 minutes
Servings: 2

Ingredients:

- 1 cup almond milk
- 2 frozen bananas
- 1/4 cup almond butter
- 4 dates, pitted
- Sliced almonds for topping

Instructions:

1. In a blender, combine almond milk, frozen bananas, almond butter, and pitted dates.
2. Blend until smooth and creamy.
3. Pour into bowls and top with sliced almonds.

Nutritional Information (per serving):
Cal: 320 | Carbs: 45g | Pro: 6g | Fat: 16g
Sugars: 29g | Fiber: 7g

18. Whole Grain Breakfast Burrito

Preparation time: 10 minutes
Servings: 2

Ingredients:

- 2 whole grain tortillas
- 4 large eggs, scrambled
- 1/2 cup black beans, drained and rinsed
- 1/2 cup salsa
- Avocado slices for garnish

Instructions:

1. In a blender, combine almond milk, frozen Warm the tortillas in a dry skillet or microwave.
2. Scramble the eggs in a pan until fully cooked.
3. Assemble the burritos by layering scrambled eggs, black beans, salsa, and avocado slices.
4. Roll the tortillas, securing the filling inside.
5. Serve immediately.

Nutritional Information (per serving):
Cal: 380 | Carbs: 40g | Pro: 19g | Fat: 15g
Sugars: 4g | Fiber: 10g

Cal: 380 | Carbs: 40g | Pro: 18g | Fat: 16g
Sugars: 3g | Fiber: 5g

19. Olive & Tomato Bruschetta

Preparation time: 10 minutes
Servings: 2

Ingredients:

- 2 slices whole grain bread, toasted
- 1/2 cup cherry tomatoes, halved
- 2 tablespoons Kalamata olives, chopped
- Fresh basil leaves, thinly sliced
- Olive oil for drizzling

Instructions:

1. Toast the whole grain bread slices.
2. In a bowl, mix cherry tomatoes, chopped Kalamata olives, and sliced basil.
3. Spoon the tomato mixture onto the toasted bread.
4. Drizzle with olive oil.
5. Serve immediately.

Nutritional Information (per serving):
Cal: 220 | Carbs: 30g | Pro: 6g | Fat: 10g
Sugars: 2g | Fiber: 5g

20. Smoked Salmon and Dill Bagel

Preparation time: 10 minutes
Servings: 2

Ingredients:

- 2 whole grain bagels, halved and toasted
- 4 oz smoked salmon
- 4 tablespoons cream cheese
- Fresh dill for garnish
- Capers for topping (optional)

Instructions:

1. Toast the whole grain bagel halves.
2. Spread cream cheese evenly on each bagel half.
3. Top with smoked salmon.
4. Garnish with fresh dill and capers if desired.
5. Serve immediately.

Nutritional Information (per serving):

First Dishes

1. Tzatziki with Pita Bread

Preparation time: 10 minutes
Servings: 2

Ingredients:

- 1 cup Greek yogurt
- 1/2 cucumber, finely diced
- 2 cloves garlic, minced
- 1 tablespoon fresh dill, chopped
- Salt to taste

Instructions:

1. In a bowl, combine Greek yogurt, diced cucumber, minced garlic, and chopped dill.
2. Mix well and add salt to taste.
3. Refrigerate for a few minutes to let the flavors meld.
4. Serve the tzatziki with fresh pita bread.

Nutritional Information (per serving):
Cal: 80 | Carbs: 7g | Pro: 10g | Fat: 1g
Sugars: 4g | Fiber: 0g

2. Baba Ganoush with Crudites

Preparation time: 10 minutes
Servings: 2

Ingredients:

- 1 large eggplant
- 2 tablespoons tahini
- 1 clove garlic, minced
- 1 tablespoon olive oil
- Salt to taste

Instructions:

1. Roast the eggplant until the skin is charred, then peel and mash the flesh.
2. In a bowl, combine mashed eggplant, tahini, minced garlic, and olive oil.
3. Mix well and add salt to taste.
4. Serve with assorted crudites.

Nutritional Information (per serving):
Cal: 120 | Carbs: 10g | Pro: 3g | Fat: 8g
Sugars: 4g | Fiber: 5g

3. Greek Fava Bean Dip (Fava)

Preparation time: 10 minutes
Servings: 2

Ingredients:

- 1 cup canned fava beans, drained
- 1 clove garlic, minced
- 2 tablespoons olive oil
- Lemon juice from 1/2 lemon
- Salt to taste

Instructions:

1. In a food processor, blend fava beans, minced garlic, olive oil, and lemon juice until smooth.
2. Add salt to taste and blend again.
3. Transfer to a serving dish.
4. Drizzle with extra olive oil and serve.

Nutritional Information (per serving):
Cal: 160 | Carbs: 18g | Pro: 5g | Fat: 9g
Sugars: 2g | Fiber: 6g

4. Mediterranean Hummus Platter

Preparation time: 10 minutes
Servings: 2

Ingredients:

- 1 cup canned chickpeas, drained
- 2 tablespoons tahini
- 1 tablespoon olive oil
- Lemon juice from 1/2 lemon
- Salt to taste

Instructions:

1. In a blender, combine chickpeas, tahini, olive oil, and lemon juice.
2. Blend until smooth, adding water if needed for a creamy consistency.
3. Season with salt to taste.
4. Arrange hummus on a platter with cherry tomatoes, cucumber slices, and olives.

Nutritional Information (per serving):
Cal: 180 | Carbs: 18g | Pro: 6g | Fat: 10g
Sugars: 3g | Fiber: 5g

5. Roasted Red Pepper and Walnut

Preparation time: 10 minutes
Servings: 2

Ingredients:

- 1 cup roasted red peppers (from a jar), drained
- 1/2 cup walnuts
- 1 clove garlic
- 2 tablespoons olive oil
- 1 teaspoon ground cumin

Instructions:

1. In a food processor, blend red peppers, walnuts, garlic, oil, & cumin until smooth.
2. Adjust seasoning as needed.
3. Transfer to a bowl.
4. Serve with pita bread or vegetable sticks.

Nutritional Information (per serving):
Cal: 220 | Carbs: 10g | Pro: 3g | Fat: 20g
Sugars: 3g | Fiber: 2g

6. Stuffed Grape Leaves (Dolma)

Preparation time: 10 minutes
Servings: 2

Ingredients:

- 10 grape leaves (from a jar), drained
- 1/2 cup cooked rice
- 2 tablespoons pine nuts
- 1 tablespoon fresh mint, chopped
- Lemon wedges for serving

Instructions:

1. In a bowl, mix cooked rice, pine nuts, and chopped mint.
2. Place a grape leaf on a flat surface, add a spoonful of the rice mixture, and roll it into a tight cylinder.
3. Repeat for all grape leaves.
4. Serve with lemon wedges.

Nutritional Information (per serving):
Cal: 180 | Carbs: 25g | Pro: 3g | Fat: 8g
Sugars: 1g | Fiber: 2g

7. Artichoke and White Bean Dip

Preparation time: 10 minutes
Servings: 2

Ingredients:

- 1 cup canned white beans, drained
- 1 cup canned artichoke hearts, drained
- 1 clove garlic, minced
- 2 tablespoons olive oil
- Salt and pepper to taste

Instructions:

1. In a food processor, blend white beans, artichoke hearts, minced garlic, and olive oil until smooth.
2. Season with salt and pepper to taste.
3. Transfer to a serving dish.
4. Serve with pita bread or vegetable sticks.

Nutritional Information (per serving):
Cal: 220 | Carbs: 25g | Pro: 7g | Fat: 11g
Sugars: 1g | Fiber: 8g

8. Caprese Salad Skewers

Preparation time: 10 minutes
Servings: 2

Ingredients:

- 12 cherry tomatoes
- 12 small fresh mozzarella balls
- Fresh basil leaves
- Balsamic glaze for drizzling
- Salt and pepper to taste

Instructions:

1. Thread a cherry tomato, a mozzarella ball, and a basil leaf onto each skewer.
2. Arrange skewers on a serving plate.
3. Drizzle with balsamic glaze.
4. Season with salt and pepper to taste.

Nutritional Information (per serving):
Cal: 150 | Carbs: 6g | Pro: 8g | Fat: 10g
Sugars: 4g | Fiber: 2g

9. Eggplant and Tomato Caponata

Preparation time: 10 minutes

Servings: 2

Ingredients:

- 1 small eggplant, diced
- 1 cup cherry tomatoes, halved
- 2 tablespoons capers
- 2 tablespoons olive oil
- Fresh parsley for garnish

Instructions:

1. In a pan, sauté diced eggplant in olive oil until golden brown.
2. Add cherry tomatoes and capers, cook until tomatoes soften.
3. Season with salt and pepper to taste.
4. Garnish with fresh parsley and serve.

Nutritional Information (per serving):
Cal: 180 | Carbs: 15g | Pro: 2g | Fat: 13g
Sugars: 8g | Fiber: 7g

10. Mediterranean Bruschetta

Preparation time: 10 minutes
Servings: 2

Ingredients:

- 4 slices whole-grain baguette
- 2 ripe tomatoes, diced
- 1/4 cup fresh basil, chopped
- 1 clove garlic, minced
- 1 tablespoon extra virgin olive oil

Instructions:

1. Toast baguette slices until golden brown.
2. In a bowl, mix diced tomatoes, chopped basil, minced garlic, and olive oil.
3. Spoon the tomato mixture onto the toasted baguette slices.
4. Serve immediately.

Nutritional Information (per serving):
Cal: 160 | Carbs: 23g | Pro: 4g | Fat: 6g
Sugars: 3g | Fiber: 4g

11. Greek Taramasalata (Fish Roe Dip)

Preparation time: 10 minutes
Servings: 2

Ingredients:

- 100g tarama (fish roe)
- 1/2 cup breadcrumbs
- 1/2 cup extra virgin olive oil
- 1 lemon, juiced
- Freshly ground black pepper, to taste

Instructions:

1. In a food processor, combine fish roe and breadcrumbs. Blend until smooth.
2. While the processor is running, slowly add olive oil until the mixture is creamy.
3. Add lemon juice and black pepper. Blend for an additional minute.
4. Transfer the dip to a serving bowl and refrigerate for 30 minutes before serving.
5. Serve with pita bread or fresh vegetables.

Nutritional Information (per serving):
Cal: 360 | Carbs: 12g | Pro: 7g | Fat: 33g
Sugars: 1g | Fiber: 1g

12. Roasted Red Pepper and Feta Dip

Preparation time: 10 minutes
Servings: 2

Ingredients:

- 1 cup roasted red peppers (from a jar), drained
- 1/2 cup feta cheese, crumbled
- 2 tablespoons extra virgin olive oil
- 1 clove garlic, minced
- Freshly ground black pepper, to taste

Instructions:

1. In a food processor, combine roasted red peppers, feta, and minced garlic.
2. Pulse until the mixture is well combined but slightly chunky.
3. While the processor is running, slowly drizzle in olive oil until smooth.
4. Add black pepper to taste.
5. Transfer the dip to a serving bowl and refrigerate for 30 minutes before serving.
6. Serve with pita chips or fresh vegetables.

Nutritional Information (per serving):
Cal: 220 | Carbs: 8g | Pro: 5g | Fat: 19g
Sugars: 4g | Fiber: 2g

13. Olive Tapenade Crostini

Preparation time: 10 minutes
Servings: 2

Ingredients:

- 1 cup mixed olives, pitted
- 2 tablespoons capers
- 2 tablespoons extra virgin olive oil
- 1 teaspoon Dijon mustard
- Baguette, sliced and toasted

Instructions:

1. In a food processor, combine olives, capers, olive oil, and Dijon mustard.
2. Pulse until the mixture forms a coarse paste.
3. Spread olive tapenade onto toasted baguette slices.
4. Serve immediately.

Nutritional Information (per serving):
Cal: 280 | Carbs: 15g | Pro: 2g | Fat: 24g
Sugars: 1g | Fiber: 3g

14. Melitzanosalata

Preparation time: 10 minutes
Servings: 2

Ingredients:

- 1 large eggplant, roasted and peeled
- 2 tablespoons extra virgin olive oil
- 1 clove garlic, minced
- 1 tablespoon red wine vinegar
- Salt and pepper, to taste

Instructions:

1. Mash the roasted eggplant in a bowl.
2. Add olive oil, minced garlic, and red wine vinegar. Mix well.
3. Season with salt and pepper to taste.
4. Refrigerate for 30 minutes before serving.
5. Serve with pita bread or as a side dish.

Nutritional Information (per serving):
Cal: 150 | Carbs: 12g | Pro: 2g | Fat: 12g
Sugars: 6g | Fiber: 5g

15. Marinated Olives with Herbs

Preparation time: 10 minutes
Servings: 2

Ingredients:

- 1 cup mixed olives
- 2 tablespoons extra virgin olive oil
- 1 teaspoon dried oregano
- 1 teaspoon dried thyme
- Zest of 1 lemon

Instructions:

1. In a bowl, toss olives with olive oil, dried oregano, dried thyme, and lemon zest.
2. Allow the olives to marinate for at least 10 minutes.
3. Serve in a bowl as a flavorful snack or appetizer.

Nutritional Information (per serving):
Cal: 180 | Carbs: 4g | Pro: 1g | Fat: 18g
Sugars: 0g | Fiber: 3g

16. Mediterranean Chickpea Salad

Preparation time: 10 minutes
Servings: 2

Ingredients:

- 1 can (15 oz) chickpeas, drained and rinsed
- 1 cucumber, diced
- 1 cup cherry tomatoes, halved
- 2 tablespoons extra virgin olive oil
- 1 tablespoon red wine vinegar
- Salt and pepper, to taste

Instructions:

1. In a bowl, combine chickpeas, diced cucumber, and halved cherry tomatoes.
2. Drizzle olive oil and red wine vinegar over the mixture.
3. Season with salt and pepper to taste.
4. Toss everything together until well combined.
5. Serve as a refreshing salad.

Nutritional Information (per serving):
Cal: 320 | Carbs: 36g | Pro: 9g | Fat: 16g
Sugars: 7g | Fiber: 10g

17. Spicy Feta & Roasted Red Pepper Dip

Preparation time: 10 minutes
Servings: 2

Ingredients:

- 1 cup feta cheese, crumbled
- 1/2 cup roasted red peppers (from a jar), drained
- 1 tablespoon extra virgin olive oil
- 1/2 teaspoon red pepper flakes
- Crackers or sliced veggies, for dipping

Instructions:

1. In a food processor, combine feta, roasted red peppers, olive oil, and red pepper flakes.
2. Pulse until the mixture is smooth and creamy.
3. Transfer the dip to a serving bowl.
4. Serve with crackers or sliced vegetables.

Nutritional Information (per serving):
Cal: 240 | Carbs: 5g | Pro: 11g | Fat: 20g
Sugars: 3g | Fiber: 1g

18. Labneh with Za'atar and Olive Oil

Preparation time: 10 minutes
Servings: 2

Ingredients:

- 1 cup labneh (strained yogurt)
- 1 teaspoon za'atar spice blend
- 1 tablespoon extra virgin olive oil
- Pita bread or crackers, for serving

Instructions:

1. Spread labneh on a serving plate.
2. Sprinkle za'atar evenly over the labneh.
3. Drizzle olive oil on top.
4. Serve with pita bread or crackers.

Nutritional Information (per serving):
Cal: 160 | Carbs: 6g | Pro: 10g | Fat: 11g
Sugars: 4g | Fiber: 0g

19. Mediterranean Antipasto Platter

Preparation time: 10 minutes
Servings: 2

Ingredients:

- 4 slices prosciutto
- 1/2 cup fresh mozzarella balls
- 1/2 cup cherry tomatoes
- 1/4 cup Kalamata olives
- 1/4 cup marinated artichoke hearts

Instructions:

1. Arrange prosciutto, mozzarella balls, cherry tomatoes, Kalamata olives, and artichoke hearts on a platter.
2. Serve as a delightful Mediterranean antipasto.

Nutritional Information (per serving):
Cal: 290 | Carbs: 6g | Pro: 16g | Fat: 23g
Sugars: 2g | Fiber: 2g

20. Greek-Style Tzatziki Deviled Eggs

Preparation time: 10 minutes
Servings: 2

Ingredients:

- 4 hard-boiled eggs, halved
- 1/2 cup Greek yogurt
- 1/4 cucumber, finely diced
- 1 tablespoon fresh dill, chopped
- Salt and pepper, to taste

Instructions:

1. Scoop out egg yolks and place them in a bowl.
2. Mash yolks with Greek yogurt, diced cucumber, and chopped fresh dill.
3. Season with salt and pepper to taste.
4. Spoon the mixture back into the egg white halves.
5. Garnish with additional dill if desired.
6. Serve chilled.

Nutritional Information (per serving):
Cal: 190 | Carbs: 6g | Pro: 17g | Fat: 11g
Sugars: 4g | Fiber: 1g

Main Courses

1. Mediterranean Baked Cod

Preparation time: 5 minutes
Servings: 2

Ingredients:

- 2 cod fillets
- 1 lemon, sliced
- 2 tablespoons olive oil
- 1 teaspoon dried oregano
- Salt and pepper to taste

Instructions:

1. Preheat the oven to 400°F (200°C).
2. Place the cod fillets on a baking sheet lined with parchment paper.
3. Drizzle olive oil over the cod fillets, ensuring they are well-coated.
4. Sprinkle dried oregano evenly over the fillets and season with salt and pepper.
5. Place lemon slices on top of each fillet.
6. Bake in the preheated oven for 8-10 minutes or until the cod is cooked through and flakes easily with a fork.
7. Serve hot, garnished with additional lemon slices if desired.

Nutritional Information (per serving):
Cal: 280 | Carbs: 3g | Pro: 30g | Fat: 16g
Sugars: 1g | Fiber: 1g

2. Grilled Chicken Souvlaki

Preparation time: 10 minutes (marination time included)
Servings: 2

Ingredients:

- 2 boneless, skinless chicken breasts, cut into cubes
- 2 tablespoons olive oil
- 2 teaspoons dried oregano
- Salt and pepper to taste
- 4 tablespoons tzatziki sauce (store-bought or homemade)

Instructions:

1. In a bowl, combine the chicken cubes, olive oil, dried oregano, salt, and pepper. Let it marinate for at least 30 minutes.
2. Preheat the grill or grill pan over medium-high heat.
3. Thread the marinated chicken cubes onto skewers.
4. Grill the chicken skewers for 5-7 minutes, turning occasionally, until fully cooked.
5. Serve the grilled chicken souvlaki with a side of tzatziki sauce for dipping.

Nutritional Information (per serving):
Cal: 320 | Carbs: 3g | Pro: 30g | Fat: 21g
Sugars: 1g | Fiber: 1g

3. Shrimp and Feta Orzo

Preparation time: 5 minutes
Servings: 2

Ingredients:

- 1 cup orzo pasta
- 8 large shrimp, peeled and deveined
- 1/2 cup crumbled feta cheese
- 2 tablespoons olive oil
- Salt and pepper to taste

Instructions:

1. Cook the orzo pasta according to package instructions. Drain and set aside.
2. In a pan, heat olive oil over medium heat. Add shrimp and cook for 2-3 minutes per side or until opaque.
3. Toss the cooked orzo with crumbled feta cheese and season with salt and pepper.
4. Top the orzo with the cooked shrimp.
5. Serve immediately.

Nutritional Information (per serving):
Cal: 410 | Carbs: 34g | Pro: 22g | Fat: 20g
Sugars: 1g | Fiber: 2g

4. Eggplant Parmesan with Sauce

Preparation time: 10 minutes
Servings: 2

Ingredients:

- 1 medium-sized eggplant, sliced into rounds
- 1 cup tomato sauce (store-bought or homemade)
- 1/2 cup shredded mozzarella cheese
- 2 tablespoons grated Parmesan cheese
- Olive oil for drizzling

Instructions:

1. Preheat the oven to 375°F (190°C).
2. Place eggplant rounds on a baking sheet.
3. Drizzle olive oil over the eggplant slices.
4. Spoon tomato sauce over each eggplant slice.
5. Sprinkle shredded mozzarella and grated Parmesan cheese over the tomato sauce.
6. Bake for 8-10 minutes or until the cheese is melted and bubbly.
7. Serve hot.

Nutritional Information (per serving):
Cal: 250 | Carbs: 15g | Pro: 12g | Fat: 16g
Sugars: 8g | Fiber: 5g

5. Lemon Herb Chicken Thighs

Preparation time: 5 minutes
Servings: 2

Ingredients:

- 4 chicken thighs, bone-in, skin-on
- 2 tablespoons olive oil
- 1 lemon, juiced
- 1 teaspoon dried thyme
- Salt and pepper to taste

Instructions:

1. Preheat the oven to 400°F (200°C).
2. In a bowl, mix together olive oil, lemon juice, dried thyme, salt, and pepper.
3. Place chicken thighs on a baking sheet.
4. Brush the chicken thighs with the lemon herb mixture, coating them evenly.
5. Roast in the preheated oven for 25-30 minutes or until the internal temperature reaches 165°F (74°C).
6. Serve hot.

Nutritional Information (per serving):
Cal: 430 | Carbs: 2g | Pro: 26g | Fat: 36g
Sugars: 1g | Fiber: 1g

6. Mediterranean Stuffed Peppers

Preparation time: 10 minutes
Servings: 2

Ingredients:

- 2 bell peppers, halved and seeds removed
- 1 cup cooked quinoa
- 1/2 cup canned chickpeas, drained and rinsed
- 1/2 cup diced tomatoes
- 2 tablespoons chopped fresh parsley

Instructions:

1. Preheat the oven to 375°F (190°C).
2. In a bowl, mix together cooked quinoa, chickpeas, diced tomatoes, and chopped parsley.
3. Stuff each bell pepper half with the quinoa mixture.
4. Place stuffed peppers on a baking sheet.
5. Bake for 20-25 minutes or until peppers are tender.
6. Serve warm.

Nutritional Information (per serving):
Cal: 300 | Carbs: 54g | Pro: 12g | Fat: 4g
Sugars: 6g | Fiber: 10g

7. Baked Falafel with Tahini Sauce

Preparation time: 10 minutes
Servings: 2

Ingredients:

- 1 can (15 oz) chickpeas, drained and rinsed
- 1/4 cup chopped fresh cilantro
- 1 teaspoon ground cumin
- Salt and pepper to taste
- Tahini sauce for serving

Instructions:

1. Preheat the oven to 375°F (190°C).
2. In a food processor, combine chickpeas, chopped cilantro, ground cumin, salt, and pepper.
3. Process until the mixture forms a coarse paste.
4. Shape the mixture into small falafel balls and place them on a baking sheet.
5. Bake for 20-25 minutes or until the falafel are golden brown.
6. Serve with tahini sauce.

Nutritional Information (per serving):
Cal: 220 | Carbs: 35g | Pro: 11g | Fat: 5g
Sugars: 7g | Fiber: 9g

8. Lemon Garlic Butter Grilled Salmon

Preparation time: 5 minutes
Servings: 2

Ingredients:

- 2 salmon fillets
- 2 tablespoons melted butter
- 2 cloves garlic, minced
- 1 lemon, juiced
- Salt and pepper to taste

Instructions:

1. Preheat the grill or grill pan over medium-high heat.
2. In a bowl, mix together melted butter, minced garlic, lemon juice, salt, and pepper.
3. Brush the salmon fillets with the lemon garlic butter mixture.
4. Grill the salmon for 3-4 minutes per side or until cooked to your liking.
5. Serve hot.

Nutritional Information (per serving):
Cal: 350 | Carbs: 1g | Pro: 25g | Fat: 27g
Sugars: 1g | Fiber: 0g

9. Chicken and Olive Tagine

Preparation time: 10 minutes
Servings: 2

Ingredients:

- 2 boneless, skinless chicken thighs
- 1 cup mixed olives (green and Kalamata)
- 1 onion, sliced
- 1 teaspoon ground cumin
- 1 teaspoon paprika

Instructions:

1. In a tagine or a deep skillet, heat olive oil over medium-high heat.
2. Brown chicken thighs on both sides.
3. Add sliced onions, ground cumin, and paprika to the tagine.
4. Add olives and a splash of water.
5. Cover and simmer for 20-25 minutes or until the chicken is cooked through.
6. Serve hot.

Nutritional Information (per serving):
Cal: 320 | Carbs: 10g | Pro: 22g | Fat: 20g
Sugars: 2g | Fiber: 4g

10. Spanakorizo

Preparation time: 10 minutes
Servings: 2

Ingredients:

- 1 cup long-grain rice
- 2 cups fresh spinach, chopped
- 1 onion, finely chopped
- 2 tablespoons olive oil
- Lemon wedges for serving

Instructions:

1. In a pot, heat olive oil over medium heat. Add chopped onions and sauté until translucent.
2. Add rice to the pot and stir for 2-3 minutes until lightly toasted.
3. Pour in 2 cups of water and bring to a boil.
4. Reduce the heat to low, add chopped spinach, cover, and simmer for 15-18 minutes or until rice is cooked.
5. Fluff the rice with a fork and serve with lemon wedges.

Nutritional Information (per serving):
Cal: 320 | Carbs: 55g | Pro: 6g | Fat: 8g
Sugars: 2g | Fiber: 3g

11. Tomato and Basil Baked Fish

Preparation time: 5 minutes
Servings: 2

Ingredients:

- 2 white fish fillets (such as tilapia or cod)
- 1 cup cherry tomatoes, halved
- 1/4 cup fresh basil, chopped
- 2 tablespoons olive oil
- Salt and pepper to taste

Instructions:

1. Preheat the oven to 400°F (200°C).
2. Place the fish fillets on a baking sheet lined with parchment paper.
3. In a bowl, mix together the cherry tomatoes,

fresh basil, olive oil, salt, and pepper.

4. Spoon the tomato and basil mixture over the fish fillets, evenly distributing it.
5. Bake in the preheated oven for 8-10 minutes or until the fish is cooked through and flakes easily with a fork.
6. Serve the baked fish with the tomato and basil topping.

Nutritional Information (per serving):
Cal: 250 | Carbs: 4g | Pro: 25g | Fat: 15g
Sugars: 2g | Fiber: 1g

12. Lamb Kofta with Mint Yogurt Sauce

Preparation time: 10 minutes
Servings: 2

Ingredients:

- 1/2 lb ground lamb
- 1 teaspoon ground cumin
- Salt and pepper to taste
- 1/2 cup Greek yogurt
- 1 tablespoon fresh mint, finely chopped

Instructions:

1. In a bowl, combine ground lamb, cumin, salt, and pepper. Mix well and form into small sausage-shaped kofta.
2. Heat a skillet over medium-high heat and cook the lamb kofta for 4-5 minutes, turning to brown on all sides.
3. In a small bowl, mix Greek yogurt with fresh mint to make the sauce.
4. Serve the lamb kofta with the mint yogurt sauce.

Nutritional Information (per serving):
Cal: 350 | Carbs: 2g | Pro: 18g | Fat: 30g
Sugars: 1g | Fiber: 0g

13. Mediterranean Quinoa Bowl

Preparation time: 10 minutes
Servings: 2

Ingredients:

- 1 cup cooked quinoa
- 1 cup mixed roasted vegetables (zucchini, bell peppers, cherry tomatoes)
- 2 tablespoons feta cheese, crumbled

- 1 tablespoon olive oil
- Fresh lemon juice to taste

Instructions:

1. In a bowl, combine cooked quinoa and mixed roasted vegetables.
2. Drizzle olive oil over the quinoa and vegetables, toss gently to coat.
3. Divide the quinoa mixture between two bowls.
4. Top each bowl with crumbled feta cheese and a squeeze of fresh lemon juice.
5. Serve immediately.

Nutritional Information (per serving):
Cal: 300 | Carbs: 35g | Pro: 8g | Fat: 15g
Sugars: 3g | Fiber: 5g

14. Chicken Piccata

Preparation time: 10 minutes
Servings: 2

Ingredients:

- 2 boneless, skinless chicken breasts
- 2 tablespoons all-purpose flour
- 2 tablespoons capers, drained
- Juice of 1 lemon
- 2 tablespoons butter

Instructions:

1. Season the chicken breasts with salt and pepper, then coat each with flour.
2. In a skillet over medium-high heat, melt the butter.
3. Add the chicken breasts and cook for 4-5 minutes on each side until golden brown.
4. Add capers and lemon juice to the skillet, letting them simmer for 1-2 minutes.
5. Serve the chicken piccata with the caper and lemon sauce.

Nutritional Information (per serving):
Cal: 400 | Carbs: 12g | Pro: 25g | Fat: 25g
Sugars: 1g | Fiber: 1g

15. Greek Moussaka

Preparation time: 10 minutes
Servings: 2

Ingredients:

- 1 eggplant, thinly sliced
- 1/2 lb ground beef or lamb
- 1 cup tomato sauce
- 1 cup béchamel sauce
- Salt and pepper to taste

Instructions:

1. Preheat the oven to 375°F (190°C).
2. In a skillet, brown the ground beef or lamb over medium heat. Season with salt and pepper.
3. Layer the sliced eggplant in a baking dish, alternating with the cooked meat.
4. Pour tomato sauce over the layers and finish with a layer of béchamel sauce.
5. Bake for 30-35 minutes or until the top is golden brown.
6. Allow the moussaka to cool for a few minutes before serving.

Nutritional Information (per serving):
Cal: 450 | Carbs: 15g | Pro: 20g | Fat: 35g
Sugars: 8g | Fiber: 5g

16. Lentil and Vegetable Stew

Preparation time: 10 minutes
Servings: 2

Ingredients:

- 1 cup cooked lentils
- 1 cup mixed vegetables (carrots, celery, bell peppers)
- 2 cups vegetable broth
- 1 teaspoon dried thyme
- Salt and pepper to taste

Instructions:

1. In a pot, combine cooked lentils, mixed vegetables, vegetable broth, thyme, salt, and pepper.
2. Bring the mixture to a boil, then reduce heat and simmer for 5-7 minutes.
3. Adjust seasoning to taste.
4. Serve the lentil and vegetable stew warm.

Nutritional Information (per serving):
Cal: 250 | Carbs: 45g | Pro: 15g | Fat: 1g
Sugars: 5g | Fiber: 15g

17. Swordfish Skewers

Preparation time: 10 minutes
Servings: 2

Ingredients:

- 2 swordfish steaks, cut into cubes
- 2 tablespoons olive oil
- Zest and juice of 1 orange
- Zest and juice of 1 lemon
- Salt and pepper to taste

Instructions:

1. In a bowl, whisk together olive oil, orange zest, orange juice, lemon zest, lemon juice, salt, and pepper.
2. Thread swordfish cubes onto skewers.
3. Brush the swordfish skewers with the citrus marinade.
4. Grill or broil the skewers for 3-4 minutes per side until the fish is cooked through.
5. Serve the swordfish skewers with additional citrus marinade.

Nutritional Information (per serving):
Cal: 300 | Carbs: 2g | Pro: 30g | Fat: 20g
Sugars: 1g | Fiber: 0g

18. Mediterranean Zucchini Noodles

Preparation time: 10 minutes
Servings: 2

Ingredients:

- 2 medium zucchinis, spiralized into noodles
- 1/4 cup store-bought or homemade pesto
- 1/4 cup cherry tomatoes, halved
- 2 tablespoons pine nuts, toasted
- Salt and pepper to taste

Instructions:

1. In a pan, sauté zucchini noodles over medium heat for 2-3 minutes until just tender.
2. Stir in pesto, cherry tomatoes, and toasted pine nuts. Cook for an additional 2 minutes.
3. Season with salt and pepper to taste.
4. Serve the Mediterranean zucchini noodles warm.

Nutritional Information (per serving):

Cal: 280 | Carbs: 10g | Pro: 5g | Fat: 25g
Sugars: 3g | Fiber: 3g

19. Beef and Eggplant Casserole

Preparation time: 10 minutes
Servings: 2

Ingredients:

- 1/2 lb ground beef
- 1 large eggplant, thinly sliced
- 1 cup tomato sauce
- 1/2 cup mozzarella cheese, shredded
- Salt and pepper to taste

Instructions:

1. Preheat the oven to 375°F (190°C).
2. In a skillet, brown the ground beef over medium heat. Season with salt and pepper.
3. In a baking dish, layer sliced eggplant, cooked ground beef, tomato sauce, and shredded mozzarella.
4. Repeat the layers, finishing with a layer of cheese on top.
5. Bake for 25-30 minutes or until the casserole is bubbly and the cheese is melted and golden.
6. Allow the casserole to cool for a few minutes before serving.

Nutritional Information (per serving):

Cal: 400 | Carbs: 15g | Pro: 20g | Fat: 30g
Sugars: 8g | Fiber: 5g

20. Stuffed Acorn Squash

Preparation time: 10 minutes
Servings: 2

Ingredients:

- 1 acorn squash, halved and seeds removed
- 1 cup cooked quinoa
- 1/2 cup chickpeas, drained and rinsed
- 1/4 cup feta cheese, crumbled
- 1 tablespoon olive oil

Instructions:

1. Preheat the oven to 375°F (190°C).
2. Place acorn squash halves on a baking sheet.
3. In a bowl, mix cooked quinoa, chickpeas, feta cheese, and olive oil.
4. Stuff each acorn squash half with the quinoa mixture.
5. Bake for 30-35 minutes or until the squash is tender.
6. Serve the stuffed acorn squash warm.

Nutritional Information (per serving):

Cal: 350 | Carbs: 45g | Pro: 10g | Fat: 15g
Sugars: 5g | Fiber: 10g

Soup

1. Greek Lemon Chicken Soup

Preparation time: 10 minutes
Servings: 2

Ingredients:

- 2 cups chicken broth
- 1/2 cup cooked chicken, shredded
- 1/2 cup orzo pasta
- 2 large eggs
- Juice of 1 lemon

Instructions:

1. In a small pot, bring the chicken broth to a gentle simmer.
2. Add the orzo pasta and shredded chicken to the simmering broth. Cook for about 7 minutes or until the orzo is tender.
3. In a bowl, whisk together the eggs and lemon juice until well combined.
4. Slowly ladle 1/2 cup of the hot broth into the egg-lemon mixture, whisking constantly to prevent curdling.
5. Gradually pour the egg-lemon mixture back into the pot, stirring continuously over low heat until the soup thickens slightly. Do not let it boil.
6. Season with salt and pepper to taste. Serve hot.

Nutritional Information (per serving):
Cal: 275 | Carbs: 23g | Pro: 20g | Fat: 11g
Sugars: 2g | Fiber: 2g

2. Tuscan White Bean Soup

Preparation time: 10 minutes
Servings: 2

Ingredients:

- 2 cups vegetable broth
- 1 can (15 oz) cannellini beans, drained and rinsed
- 1 cup cherry tomatoes, halved
- 2 cloves garlic, minced
- 1 teaspoon dried Italian herbs

Instructions:

1. In a saucepan, combine the vegetable broth, cannellini beans, cherry tomatoes, minced garlic, and dried Italian herbs.

2. Bring the mixture to a simmer over medium heat, stirring occasionally, for about 5 minutes.
3. Season with salt and pepper to taste. Serve hot.

Nutritional Information (per serving):
Cal: 230 | Carbs: 40g | Pro: 15g | Fat: 1g
Sugars: 3g | Fiber: 10g

3. Tomato and Red Lentil Soup

Preparation time: 10 minutes
Servings: 2

Ingredients:

- 2 cups vegetable broth
- 1/2 cup red lentils, rinsed
- 1 can (14 oz) diced tomatoes
- 1 teaspoon ground cumin
- Salt and pepper to taste

Instructions:

1. In a pot, combine the vegetable broth, red lentils, diced tomatoes, and ground cumin.
2. Bring the mixture to a boil, then reduce heat and simmer for 7-8 minutes or until lentils are tender.
3. Season with salt and pepper to taste. Serve hot.

Nutritional Information (per serving):
Cal: 280 | Carbs: 50g | Pro: 16g | Fat: 2g
Sugars: 6g | Fiber: 17g

4. Mediterranean Vegetable Soup

Preparation time: 10 minutes
Servings: 2

Ingredients:

- 2 cups vegetable broth
- 1 zucchini, diced
- 1 red bell pepper, diced
- 1 cup cherry tomatoes, halved
- 1 tablespoon olive oil
- Fresh basil for garnish

Instructions:

1. In a pot, heat olive oil over medium heat.

2. Add diced zucchini and red bell pepper. Sauté for 3-4 minutes.
3. Add vegetable broth and cherry tomatoes to the pot. Bring to a simmer and cook for an additional 5 minutes.
4. Season with salt and pepper to taste. Garnish with fresh basil. Serve hot.

Nutritional Information (per serving):
Cal: 120 | Carbs: 14g | Pro: 2g | Fat: 7g
Sugars: 8g | Fiber: 4g

5. Fasolada (Greek Bean Soup)

Preparation time: 10 minutes
Servings: 2

Ingredients:

- 2 cups vegetable broth
- 1 can (15 oz) cannellini beans, drained and rinsed
- 1 onion, chopped
- 2 tablespoons olive oil
- 1 teaspoon dried oregano

Instructions:

1. In a pot, heat olive oil over medium heat. Add chopped onion and sauté until translucent.
2. Add vegetable broth, cannellini beans, and dried oregano. Bring to a simmer and cook for 5-6 minutes.
3. Season with salt and pepper to taste. Serve hot.

Nutritional Information (per serving):
Cal: 290 | Carbs: 45g | Pro: 13g | Fat: 7g
Sugars: 4g | Fiber: 13g

6. Spicy Chickpea and Tomato Soup

Preparation time: 10 minutes
Servings: 2

Ingredients:

- 2 cups vegetable broth
- 1 can (15 oz) chickpeas, drained and rinsed
- 1 cup crushed tomatoes
- 1 teaspoon smoked paprika
- Fresh cilantro for garnish

Instructions:

1. In a pot, combine vegetable broth, chickpeas, crushed tomatoes, smoked paprika.
2. Bring the mixture to a boil, then reduce heat and simmer for 5-6 minutes.
3. Season with salt and pepper to taste. Garnish with fresh cilantro. Serve hot.

Nutritional Information (per serving):
Cal: 210 | Carbs: 36g | Pro: 10g | Fat: 3g
Sugars: 8g | Fiber: 10g

7. Minestrone Soup

Preparation time: 10 minutes
Servings: 2

Ingredients:

- 2 cups vegetable broth
- 1/2 cup whole wheat pasta
- 1 can (14 oz) diced tomatoes
- 1 cup mixed vegetables (carrots, celery, zucchini)
- 1 teaspoon dried Italian herbs

Instructions:

1. In a pot, combine vegetable broth, whole wheat pasta, diced tomatoes, and mixed vegetables.
2. Bring the mixture to a boil, then reduce heat and simmer for 7-8 minutes or until pasta is cooked.
3. Season with salt and pepper to taste. Serve hot.

Nutritional Information (per serving):
Cal: 250 | Carbs: 47g | Pro: 10g | Fat: 2g
Sugars: 8g | Fiber: 10g

8. Roasted Red Pepper

Preparation time: 10 minutes
Servings: 2

Ingredients:

- 2 cups tomato soup
- 1/2 cup roasted red peppers, drained
- 1/2 cup unsweetened almond milk
- 1 tablespoon olive oil

- Fresh basil for garnish

Instructions:

1. In a blender, combine tomato soup, roasted red peppers, almond milk, and olive oil. Blend until smooth.
2. Pour the mixture into a pot and heat over medium heat until warmed through.
3. Season with salt and pepper to taste. Garnish with fresh basil. Serve hot.

Nutritional Information (per serving):
Cal: 180 | Carbs: 20g | Pro: 4g | Fat: 11g
Sugars: 10g | Fiber: 3g

9. Lemon and Spinach Orzo Soup

Preparation time: 10 minutes
Servings: 2

Ingredients:

- 2 cups vegetable broth
- 1/2 cup orzo pasta
- 1 cup fresh spinach
- Juice of 1 lemon
- 1 tablespoon olive oil

Instructions:

1. In a pot, bring vegetable broth to a boil. Add orzo pasta and cook for 7-8 minutes or until tender.
2. Stir in fresh spinach until wilted. Add lemon juice and olive oil.
3. Season with salt and pepper to taste. Serve hot.

Nutritional Information (per serving):
Cal: 230 | Carbs: 40g | Pro: 6g | Fat: 6g
Sugars: 2g | Fiber: 2g

10. Harira (Lentil and Chickpea Soup)

Preparation time: 10 minutes
Servings: 2

Ingredients:

- 2 cups vegetable broth
- 1/2 cup red lentils, rinsed
- 1 can (15 oz) chickpeas, drained and rinsed
- 1/2 cup diced tomatoes

- 1 teaspoon ground cumin

Instructions:

1. In a pot, combine vegetable broth, red lentils, chickpeas, diced tomatoes, and ground cumin.
2. Bring the mixture to a boil, then reduce heat and simmer for 7-8 minutes or until lentils are tender.
3. Season with salt and pepper to taste. Serve hot.

Nutritional Information (per serving):
Cal: 260 | Carbs: 45g | Pro: 14g | Fat: 3g
Sugars: 6g | Fiber: 17g

11. Mediterranean Fish Soup

Preparation time: 5 minutes
Servings: 2

Ingredients:

- 1 cup cherry tomatoes, halved
- 200g white fish fillets, cut into bite-sized pieces
- 2 cups vegetable broth
- 1 tablespoon olive oil
- 1 teaspoon dried oregano

Instructions:

1. In a pot, heat olive oil over medium heat.
2. Add cherry tomatoes and cook for 2 minutes until slightly softened.
3. Pour in the vegetable broth and bring it to a simmer.
4. Add the fish pieces and oregano. Cook for an additional 5 minutes or until the fish is cooked through.
5. Serve the soup hot, and if desired, garnish with a drizzle of olive oil.

Nutritional Information (per serving):
Cal: 175 | Carbs: 6g | Pro: 20g | Fat: 9g
Sugars: 3g | Fiber: 2g

12. Wedding Soup with Meatballs

Preparation time: 10 minutes
Servings: 2

Ingredients:

- 4 cups chicken broth
- 200g ground turkey
- 1/2 cup acini di pepe pasta
- 1 cup fresh spinach, chopped
- Salt and pepper to taste

Instructions:

1. In a pot, bring chicken broth to a simmer.
2. In a bowl, season ground turkey with salt and pepper. Form small meatballs and drop them into the simmering broth.
3. Add acini di pepe pasta and cook for 5 minutes until meatballs are cooked through and pasta is tender.
4. Stir in chopped spinach and cook for an additional 2 minutes until wilted.
5. Serve the soup hot.

Nutritional Information (per serving):
Cal: 240 | Carbs: 23g | Pro: 24g | Fat: 7g
Sugars: 1g | Fiber: 2g

13. Greek Lentil Soup

Preparation time: 10 minutes
Servings: 2

Ingredients:

- 1 cup dry green lentils
- 4 cups vegetable broth
- 1 onion, finely chopped
- 2 cloves garlic, minced
- 1 tablespoon olive oil

Instructions:

1. Rinse lentils under cold water.
2. In a pot, sauté chopped onion and garlic in olive oil until softened.
3. Add lentils and vegetable broth. Bring to a boil, then reduce heat and simmer for 8 minutes.
4. Serve the soup hot, drizzled with a bit of olive oil if desired.

Nutritional Information (per serving):
Cal: 320 | Carbs: 52g | Pro: 21g | Fat: 5g
Sugars: 5g | Fiber: 25g

14. Chickpea and Vegetable Stew

Preparation time: 10 minutes

Servings: 2

Ingredients:

- 1 can (15 oz) chickpeas, drained and rinsed
- 1 cup cherry tomatoes, halved
- 1 zucchini, diced
- 1 cup vegetable broth
- 1 teaspoon dried Italian herbs

Instructions:

1. In a pot, combine chickpeas, cherry tomatoes, zucchini, vegetable broth, and Italian herbs.
2. Bring to a simmer and cook for 8 minutes until vegetables are tender.
3. Serve the stew hot.

Nutritional Information (per serving):
Cal: 240 | Carbs: 42g | Pro: 12g | Fat: 4g
Sugars: 9g | Fiber: 12g

15. Cannellini Bean and Kale Soup

Preparation time: 10 minutes
Servings: 2

Ingredients:

- 1 can (15 oz) cannellini beans, drained and rinsed
- 2 cups kale, chopped
- 4 cups vegetable broth
- 2 cloves garlic, minced
- 1 tablespoon olive oil

Instructions:

1. In a pot, sauté minced garlic in olive oil until fragrant.
2. Add cannellini beans, kale, and vegetable broth. Bring to a simmer and cook for 5 minutes.
3. Serve the soup hot.

Nutritional Information (per serving):
Cal: 180 | Carbs: 30g | Pro: 10g | Fat: 4g
Sugars: 3g | Fiber: 8g

16. Gazpacho with Mediterranean Twist

Preparation time: 10 minutes
Servings: 2

Ingredients:

- 4 large tomatoes, chopped
- 1 cucumber, peeled and chopped
- 1 red bell pepper, chopped
- 2 cups tomato juice
- 2 tablespoons olive oil

Instructions:

1. In a blender, combine chopped tomatoes, cucumber, red bell pepper, tomato juice, and olive oil.
2. Blend until smooth.
3. Chill the gazpacho in the refrigerator for at least 30 minutes before serving.
4. Serve the soup cold.

Nutritional Information (per serving):
Cal: 180 | Carbs: 20g | Pro: 3g | Fat: 12g
Sugars: 12g | Fiber: 5g

17. Avgolemono Orzo & Chicken Soup

Preparation time: 10 minutes
Servings: 2

Ingredients:

- 2 cups chicken broth
- 1/2 cup orzo pasta
- 1 cup cooked chicken, shredded
- 2 eggs
- Juice of 1 lemon

Instructions:

1. In a pot, bring chicken broth to a boil.
2. Add orzo pasta and cooked chicken. Cook for 5 minutes until pasta is tender.
3. In a bowl, whisk together eggs and lemon juice.
4. Slowly pour the egg mixture into the soup, stirring continuously.
5. Serve the soup hot.

Nutritional Information (per serving):
Cal: 300 | Carbs: 27g | Pro: 24g | Fat: 10g
Sugars: 1g | Fiber: 2g

18. Spinach and Lentil Soup

Preparation time: 10 minutes
Servings: 2

Ingredients:

- 1 cup dry red lentils
- 4 cups vegetable broth
- 2 cups fresh spinach, chopped
- 1 onion, finely chopped
- 1 tablespoon olive oil

Instructions:

1. Rinse red lentils under cold water.
2. In a pot, sauté chopped onion in olive oil until softened.
3. Add red lentils and vegetable broth. Bring to a boil, then reduce heat and simmer for 8 minutes.
4. Stir in chopped spinach and cook for an additional 2 minutes until wilted.
5. Serve the soup hot.

Nutritional Information (per serving):
Cal: 280 | Carbs: 45g | Pro: 18g | Fat: 4g
Sugars: 4g | Fiber: 16g

19. Roasted Eggplant & Tomato Soup

Preparation time: 10 minutes
Servings: 2

Ingredients:

- 1 eggplant, diced
- 1 cup cherry tomatoes, halved
- 2 cups vegetable broth
- 2 cloves garlic, minced
- 1 tablespoon olive oil

Instructions:

1. Preheat the oven to 400°F (200°C).
2. Toss diced eggplant and cherry tomatoes with minced garlic and olive oil. Roast in the oven for 8 minutes.
3. In a pot, heat vegetable broth and add the roasted vegetables. Simmer for 2 minutes.
4. Serve the soup hot.

Nutritional Information (per serving):
Cal: 200 | Carbs: 28g | Pro: 4g | Fat: 9g
Sugars: 12g | Fiber: 9g

20. Moroccan Spiced Carrot Soup

Preparation time: 10 minutes

Servings: 2

Ingredients:

- 4 large carrots, chopped
- 1 onion, chopped
- 4 cups vegetable broth
- 1 teaspoon Moroccan spice blend
- 1 tablespoon olive oil

Instructions:

1. In a pot, sauté chopped onion in olive oil until softened.
2. Add chopped carrots, vegetable broth, and Moroccan spice blend. Bring to a boil, then reduce heat and simmer for 8 minutes.
3. Blend the soup until smooth using a blender or immersion blender.
4. Serve the soup hot.

Nutritional Information (per serving):
Cal: 160 | Carbs: 28g | Pro: 2g | Fat: 5g
Sugars: 12g | Fiber: 8g

Poultry

1. Greek Chicken Souvlaki Skewers

Preparation time: 10 minutes
Servings: 2

Ingredients:

- 1 lb boneless, skinless chicken breasts, cut into cubes
- 2 tablespoons olive oil
- 1 tablespoon dried oregano
- Juice of 1 lemon
- Salt and pepper to taste

Instructions:

1. In a bowl, combine olive oil, dried oregano, lemon juice, salt, and pepper. Mix well to create the marinade.
2. Add the chicken cubes to the marinade, ensuring they are well-coated. Let it marinate for 5 minutes.
3. Thread the marinated chicken onto skewers.
4. Preheat a grill or grill pan over medium-high heat.
5. Grill the chicken skewers for 4-5 minutes on each side or until fully cooked.
6. Serve the Greek Chicken Souvlaki Skewers with a side of Greek salad or pita bread.

Nutritional Information (per serving):
Cal: 350 | Carbs: 2g | Pro: 38g | Fat: 20g
Sugars: 0g | Fiber: 1g

2. Lemon Garlic Roast Chicken

Preparation time: 10 minutes
Servings: 2

Ingredients:

- 2 bone-in, skin-on chicken thighs
- 3 tablespoons olive oil
- 4 cloves garlic, minced
- 1 lemon, sliced
- Salt and pepper to taste

Instructions:

1. Preheat the oven to 400°F (200°C).
2. Rub chicken thighs with olive oil, minced garlic, salt, and pepper.
3. Place the chicken in a baking dish and arrange lemon slices on top.
4. Roast in the preheated oven for 30-35 minutes or until the chicken reaches an internal temperature of 165°F (74°C).
5. Serve the Lemon Garlic Roast Chicken with your favorite roasted vegetables or a simple salad.

Nutritional Information (per serving):
Cal: 420 | Carbs: 4g | Pro: 22g | Fat: 35g
Sugars: 0g | Fiber: 1g

3. Mediterranean Chicken & Olive Tagine

Preparation time: 10 minutes
Servings: 2

Ingredients:

- 1 lb chicken thighs, bone-in, skin-on
- 1 cup mixed olives (green and Kalamata)
- 2 tablespoons olive oil
- 2 teaspoons dried oregano
- Salt and pepper to taste

Instructions:

1. In a tagine or a deep skillet, heat olive oil over medium-high heat.
2. Season chicken thighs with dried oregano, salt, and pepper.
3. Place chicken in the tagine and brown on both sides.
4. Add mixed olives to the tagine and cook for an additional 5 minutes.
5. Cover and simmer on low heat for 20-25 minutes or until the chicken is fully cooked.
6. Serve the Mediterranean Chicken and Olive Tagine with couscous or crusty bread.

Nutritional Information (per serving):
Cal: 480 | Carbs: 5g | Pro: 24g | Fat: 40g
Sugars: 0g | Fiber: 2g

4. Baked Lemon Herb Chicken Thighs

Preparation time: 10 minutes
Servings: 2

Ingredients:

- 2 chicken thighs, bone-in, skin-on
- 2 tablespoons olive oil
- 1 tablespoon dried mixed herbs (rosemary, thyme, sage)
- Juice of 1 lemon

- Salt and pepper to taste

Instructions:

1. Preheat the oven to 375°F (190°C).
2. Rub chicken thighs with olive oil, dried herbs, lemon juice, salt, and pepper.
3. Place the chicken in a baking dish.
4. Bake for 35-40 minutes or until the chicken reaches an internal temperature of 165°F (74°C).
5. Serve the Baked Lemon Herb Chicken Thighs with steamed vegetables or a simple salad.

Nutritional Information (per serving):
Cal: 380 | Carbs: 1g | Pro: 24g | Fat: 32g
Sugars: 0g | Fiber: 0g

5. Chicken Gyro Wrap with Tzatziki

Preparation time: 10 minutes
Servings: 2

Ingredients:

- 1 lb boneless, skinless chicken breasts, thinly sliced
- 1 cup plain Greek yogurt
- 2 tablespoons olive oil
- 1 teaspoon dried oregano
- 2 whole wheat wraps

Instructions:

1. In a bowl, mix sliced chicken with olive oil and dried oregano.
2. Cook the chicken in a skillet over medium-high heat until fully cooked.
3. Warm the whole wheat wraps.
4. In a separate bowl, mix Greek yogurt with a pinch of salt to make tzatziki.
5. Assemble the wraps by placing cooked chicken in the center, drizzling with tzatziki, and rolling them up.
6. Serve the Chicken Gyro Wraps with a side of Greek salad.

Nutritional Information (per serving):
Cal: 420 | Carbs: 20g | Pro: 40g | Fat: 20g
Sugars: 5g | Fiber: 3g

6. Grilled Rosemary Lemon Chicken

Preparation time: 10 minutes
Servings: 2

Ingredients:

- 2 chicken breasts, boneless, skinless
- 2 tablespoons olive oil
- 1 tablespoon fresh rosemary, chopped
- Juice of 1 lemon
- Salt and pepper to taste

Instructions:

1. Preheat a grill or grill pan over medium-high heat.
2. Rub chicken breasts with olive oil, chopped rosemary, lemon juice, salt, and pepper.
3. Grill the chicken for 5-6 minutes on each side or until fully cooked.
4. Let the chicken rest for a few minutes before slicing.
5. Serve the Grilled Rosemary Lemon Chicken Breasts with a side of roasted vegetables or quinoa.

Nutritional Information (per serving):
Cal: 320 | Carbs: 2g | Pro: 40g | Fat: 16g
Sugars: 0g | Fiber: 1g

7. Chicken Piccata with Artichokes

Preparation time: 10 minutes
Servings: 2

Ingredients:

- 2 chicken breasts, boneless, skinless
- 2 tablespoons olive oil
- 1/4 cup capers, drained
- Juice of 2 lemons
- Salt and pepper to taste

Instructions:

1. Season chicken breasts with salt and pepper.
2. In a skillet, heat olive oil over medium-high heat.
3. Cook chicken breasts for 4-5 minutes on each side or until fully cooked.
4. Add capers and lemon juice to the skillet, allowing them to simmer for 2 minutes.
5. Serve the Chicken Piccata with Artichokes over a bed of whole wheat pasta or steamed asparagus.

Nutritional Information (per serving):
Cal: 320 | Carbs: 2g | Pro: 40g | Fat: 16g
Sugars: 0g | Fiber: 1g

8. Greek Lemon Chicken with Potatoes

Preparation time: 10 minutes
Servings: 2

Ingredients:

- 2 chicken thighs, bone-in, skin-on
- 2 large potatoes, peeled and cut into chunks
- 3 tablespoons olive oil
- Juice of 1 lemon
- Salt and pepper to taste

Instructions:

1. Preheat the oven to 400°F (200°C).
2. In a bowl, mix chicken thighs, potato chunks, olive oil, lemon juice, salt, and pepper.
3. Place the chicken and potatoes in a baking dish.
4. Bake for 45-50 minutes or until the chicken is fully cooked, and the potatoes are golden.
5. Serve the Greek Lemon Chicken with Potatoes with a side of Greek salad.

Nutritional Information (per serving):

Cal: 480 | Carbs: 30g | Pro: 22g | Fat: 30g
Sugars: 2g | Fiber: 4g

9. Chicken & Spinach Stuffed Bell Peppers

Preparation time: 10 minutes
Servings: 2

Ingredients:

- 2 bell peppers, halved and seeds removed
- 1 cup cooked shredded chicken
- 1 cup fresh spinach, chopped
- 1/2 cup feta cheese, crumbled
- Salt and pepper to taste

Instructions:

1. Preheat the oven to 375°F (190°C).
2. In a bowl, mix shredded chicken, chopped spinach, crumbled feta, salt, and pepper.
3. Stuff each bell pepper half with the chicken and spinach mixture.
4. Bake for 20-25 minutes or until the peppers are tender.
5. Serve the Chicken and Spinach Stuffed Bell Peppers with a side of quinoa or couscous.

Nutritional Information (per serving):

Cal: 280 | Carbs: 16g | Pro: 25g | Fat: 14g
Sugars: 8g | Fiber: 4g

10. Moroccan Chicken

Preparation time: 10 minutes
Servings: 2

Ingredients:

- 2 chicken thighs, bone-in, skin-on
- 1/2 cup dried apricots, chopped
- 1/4 cup slivered almonds
- 2 tablespoons olive oil
- 1 teaspoon ground cinnamon

Instructions:

1. Preheat the oven to 375°F (190°C).
2. In a bowl, mix dried apricots, slivered almonds, olive oil, and ground cinnamon.
3. Rub chicken thighs with the apricot and almond mixture.
4. Place the chicken in a baking dish and bake for 35-40 minutes or until fully cooked.
5. Serve the Moroccan Chicken with Apricots and Almonds over a bed of couscous.

Nutritional Information (per serving):

Cal: 380 | Carbs: 18g | Pro: 22g | Fat: 26g
Sugars: 14g | Fiber: 3g

11. Mediterranean Chicken Pita Sandwich

Preparation time: 10 minutes
Servings: 2

Ingredients:

- 2 boneless, skinless chicken breasts
- 1 teaspoon dried oregano
- 2 whole wheat pita bread
- 1 cup cherry tomatoes, halved
- 1/2 cucumber, thinly sliced

Instructions:

1. Preheat a grill or grill pan over medium-high heat.
2. Season the chicken breasts with dried oregano, salt, and pepper.
3. Grill the chicken for 4-5 minutes per side or until cooked through.
4. While the chicken is cooking, warm the pita

bread in the grill or on a stovetop.
5. Slice the grilled chicken into thin strips.
6. Assemble the pita sandwiches by placing sliced chicken, cherry tomatoes, and cucumber inside the warm pita bread.
7. Serve immediately and enjoy your Mediterranean Chicken Pita Sandwich!

Nutritional Information (per serving):
Cal: 350 | Carbs: 34g | Pro: 35g | Fat: 8g
Sugars: 5g | Fiber: 6g

12. Baked Harissa Chicken Thighs

Preparation time: 10 minutes
Servings: 2

Ingredients:

- 4 bone-in, skin-on chicken thighs
- 2 tablespoons harissa paste
- 1 tablespoon olive oil
- Salt and pepper, to taste

Instructions:

1. Preheat the oven to 400°F (200°C).
2. In a small bowl, mix harissa paste and olive oil to create a marinade.
3. Place the chicken thighs on a baking sheet lined with parchment paper.
4. Season chicken thighs with salt and pepper, then brush them with the harissa marinade.
5. Bake for 25-30 minutes or until the chicken reaches an internal temperature of 165°F (74°C).
6. Remove from the oven and let it rest for a few minutes before serving.

Nutritional Information (per serving):
Cal: 420 | Carbs: 1g | Pro: 30g | Fat: 33g
Sugars: 0g | Fiber: 0g

13. Chicken Kebabs with Yogurt Marinade

Preparation time: 10 minutes
Servings: 2

Ingredients:

- 2 boneless, skinless chicken breasts, cut into cubes
- 1/2 cup plain Greek yogurt
- 1 tablespoon olive oil

- 1 teaspoon ground cumin
- Salt and pepper, to taste

Instructions:

1. In a bowl, mix Greek yogurt, olive oil, ground cumin, salt, and pepper to create the marinade.
2. Thread the chicken cubes onto skewers.
3. Brush the chicken kebabs with the yogurt marinade.
4. Grill the kebabs for 4-5 minutes per side or until fully cooked.
5. Serve immediately and enjoy the flavorful Chicken Kebabs!

Nutritional Information (per serving):
Cal: 280 | Carbs: 3g | Pro: 38g | Fat: 12g
Sugars: 2g | Fiber: 0g

14. Italian Herb Roasted Turkey Breast

Preparation time: 10 minutes
Servings: 2

Ingredients:

- 2 turkey breast slices
- 1 tablespoon dried Italian herbs
- 2 tablespoons olive oil
- Salt and pepper, to taste

Instructions:

1. Preheat the oven to 375°F (190°C).
2. Place turkey breast slices on a baking sheet lined with parchment paper.
3. Drizzle olive oil over the turkey slices.
4. Season with dried Italian herbs, salt, and pepper.
5. Roast in the oven for 20-25 minutes or until the turkey reaches an internal temperature of 165°F (74°C).
6. Let it rest for a few minutes before slicing and serving.

Nutritional Information (per serving):
Cal: 220 | Carbs: 0g | Pro: 40g | Fat: 6g
Sugars: 0g | Fiber: 0g

15. Lemon Oregano Chicken Skillet

Preparation time: 10 minutes
Servings: 2

Ingredients:

- 2 boneless, skinless chicken breasts
- 1 lemon, juiced
- 2 tablespoons olive oil
- 1 teaspoon dried oregano
- Salt and pepper, to taste

Instructions:

1. Season chicken breasts with dried oregano, salt, and pepper.
2. In a skillet, heat olive oil over medium-high heat.
3. Add chicken breasts to the skillet and cook for 4-5 minutes per side or until fully cooked.
4. Pour lemon juice over the chicken during the last few minutes of cooking.
5. Serve the Lemon Oregano Chicken hot from the skillet.

Nutritional Information (per serving):
Cal: 320 | Carbs: 2g | Pro: 35g | Fat: 18g
Sugars: 0g | Fiber: 0g

16. Chicken and Vegetable Kabobs

Preparation time: 10 minutes
Servings: 2

Ingredients:

- 2 boneless, skinless chicken breasts, cut into cubes
- 1 bell pepper, cut into chunks
- 1 zucchini, sliced
- 1 red onion, cut into wedges
- 2 tablespoons olive oil
- Salt and pepper, to taste

Instructions:

1. Preheat a grill or grill pan over medium-high heat.
2. Thread chicken, bell pepper, zucchini, and red onion alternately onto skewers.
3. Brush the kabobs with olive oil and season with salt and pepper.
4. Grill for 4-5 minutes per side or until the chicken is cooked through.
5. Serve the Chicken and Vegetable Kabobs hot off the grill.

Nutritional Information (per serving):
Cal: 280 | Carbs: 10g | Pro: 30g | Fat: 14g

Sugars: 5g | Fiber: 3g

17. Mediterranean Chicken & Couscous

Preparation time: 10 minutes
Servings: 2

Ingredients:

- 1 cup cooked couscous
- 2 boneless, skinless chicken breasts, cooked and shredded
- 1 cup cherry tomatoes, halved
- 1/4 cup feta cheese, crumbled
- 2 tablespoons olive oil

Instructions:

1. In a large bowl, combine cooked couscous, shredded chicken, cherry tomatoes, and feta cheese.
2. Drizzle olive oil over the salad and toss until well combined.
3. Serve the Mediterranean Chicken and Couscous Salad chilled or at room temperature.

Nutritional Information (per serving):
Cal: 380 | Carbs: 33g | Pro: 25g | Fat: 18g
Sugars: 3g | Fiber: 3g

18. Chicken Shawarma Bowl

Preparation time: 10 minutes
Servings: 2

Ingredients:

- 2 boneless, skinless chicken thighs
- 2 tablespoons Shawarma spice blend
- 1 cup cooked quinoa
- 1 cup cucumber, diced
- 1/4 cup tahini sauce

Instructions:

1. Rub Shawarma spice blend onto chicken thighs.
2. Grill or pan-sear the chicken for 4-5 minutes per side or until fully cooked.
3. Slice the chicken into strips.
4. In bowls, assemble quinoa, diced cucumber, and sliced chicken.
5. Drizzle tahini sauce over the top.
6. Serve the Chicken Shawarma Bowl

immediately.

Nutritional Information (per serving):
Cal: 450 | Carbs: 33g | Pro: 25g | Fat: 25g
Sugars: 3g | Fiber: 4g

19. Mediterranean Chicken Pasta

Preparation time: 10 minutes
Servings: 2

Ingredients:

- 200g whole wheat pasta
- 2 boneless, skinless chicken breasts, cooked and sliced
- 1/2 cup sun-dried tomatoes, chopped
- 2 tablespoons olive oil
- 2 tablespoons grated Parmesan cheese

Instructions:

1. Cook the pasta according to package instructions.
2. In a skillet, heat olive oil over medium heat.
3. Add cooked chicken slices and sun-dried tomatoes, sauté for 2-3 minutes.
4. Toss the cooked pasta into the skillet and mix well.
5. Divide the Mediterranean Chicken Pasta between two plates.
6. Sprinkle grated Parmesan cheese on top and serve.

Nutritional Information (per serving):
Cal: 480 | Carbs: 54g | Pro: 35g | Fat: 16g
Sugars: 5g | Fiber: 8g

20. Lemon Za'atar Grilled Chicken

Preparation time: 10 minutes
Servings: 2

Ingredients:

- 4 chicken drumsticks
- Zest and juice of 1 lemon
- 2 tablespoons Za'atar spice blend
- 2 tablespoons olive oil
- Salt and pepper, to taste

Instructions:

1. Preheat a grill or grill pan over medium-high heat.
2. In a bowl, mix together lemon zest, lemon juice, Za'atar spice blend, olive oil, salt, and pepper.
3. Rub the lemon Za'atar mixture onto the chicken drumsticks.
4. Grill the drumsticks for 15-20 minutes, turning occasionally, until fully cooked.
5. Serve the Lemon Za'atar Grilled Chicken Drumsticks hot off the grill.

Nutritional Information (per serving):
Cal: 360 | Carbs: 1g | Pro: 32g | Fat: 25g
Sugars: 0g | Fiber: 0g

Pork and Beef

1. Greek Lamb and Beef Gyros

Preparation time: 10 minutes
Servings: 2

Ingredients:

- 200g ground lamb
- 200g ground beef
- 1 tablespoon Greek seasoning
- 2 pita bread
- Tzatziki sauce for serving

Instructions:

1. In a bowl, mix ground lamb and beef with Greek seasoning.
2. Form small, thin patties with the mixture.
3. Heat a skillet over medium-high heat and cook patties for 3-4 minutes per side until cooked through.
4. Warm pita bread in the skillet for 1 minute.
5. Place gyros patties on pita bread and serve with tzatziki sauce.

Nutritional Information (per serving):
Cal: 550 | Carbs: 22g | Pro: 30g | Fat: 38g
Sugars: 1g | Fiber: 2g

2. Mediterranean Beef & Spinach Stuffed Peppers

Preparation time: 10 minutes
Servings: 2

Ingredients:

- 2 large bell peppers, halved and seeds removed
- 300g ground beef
- 1 cup fresh spinach, chopped
- 1 cup cooked quinoa
- Salt and pepper to taste

Instructions:

1. Preheat oven to 375°F (190°C).
2. In a skillet, brown ground beef over medium heat, then add chopped spinach and cook until wilted.
3. Season beef and spinach mixture with salt and pepper.
4. In a bowl, mix cooked quinoa with the beef and spinach.
5. Stuff the halved bell peppers with the mixture.

6. Bake for 20 minutes or until peppers are tender.

Nutritional Information (per serving):
Cal: 480 | Carbs: 34g | Pro: 28g | Fat: 24g
Sugars: 5g | Fiber: 7g

3. Baked Lamb Meatballs

Preparation time: 10 minutes
Servings: 2

Ingredients:

- 250g ground lamb
- 1/4 cup breadcrumbs
- 1 teaspoon dried mint
- Salt and pepper to taste
- 1/2 cup Greek yogurt for the sauce

Instructions:

1. Preheat the oven to 400°F (200°C).
2. In a bowl, combine ground lamb, breadcrumbs, dried mint, salt, and pepper.
3. Form small meatballs and place them on a baking sheet.
4. Bake for 15 minutes or until cooked through.
5. Mix Greek yogurt with a pinch of dried mint for the sauce.
6. Serve baked lamb meatballs with mint yogurt sauce.

Nutritional Information (per serving):
Cal: 480 | Carbs: 9g | Pro: 27g | Fat: 38g
Sugars: 3g | Fiber: 1g

4. Pork Souvlaki with Lemon & Oregano

Preparation time: 10 minutes
Servings: 2

Ingredients:

- 300g pork loin, cut into cubes
- 2 tablespoons olive oil
- 1 lemon, juiced
- 1 teaspoon dried oregano
- Salt and pepper to taste

Instructions:

1. In a bowl, mix pork cubes with olive oil, lemon juice, dried oregano, salt, and pepper.

2. Thread the pork onto skewers.
3. Grill skewers on medium-high heat for 5 minutes, turning occasionally.
4. Serve with a squeeze of lemon.

Nutritional Information (per serving):
Cal: 420 | Carbs: 2g | Pro: 28g | Fat: 33g
Sugars: 1g | Fiber: 1g

5. Beef and Eggplant Moussaka

Preparation time: 10 minutes
Servings: 2

Ingredients:

- 300g ground beef
- 1 large eggplant, thinly sliced
- 1 cup tomato sauce
- 1/2 cup grated Parmesan cheese
- Salt and pepper to taste

Instructions:

1. Preheat oven to 375°F (190°C).
2. In a skillet, brown ground beef and season with salt and pepper.
3. Layer eggplant slices in a baking dish, alternating with ground beef and tomato sauce.
4. Repeat layers, finishing with a layer of eggplant on top.
5. Sprinkle Parmesan cheese over the top layer.
6. Bake for 30 minutes or until eggplant is tender and the top is golden.

Nutritional Information (per serving):
Cal: 480 | Carbs: 24g | Pro: 26g | Fat: 33g
Sugars: 11g | Fiber: 9g

6. Mediterranean Lamb Kofta Burgers

Preparation time: 10 minutes
Servings: 2

Ingredients:

- 250g ground lamb
- 1 teaspoon ground cumin
- 1/2 teaspoon ground coriander
- Salt and pepper to taste
- 2 whole grain burger buns

Instructions:

1. In a bowl, combine ground lamb with cumin, coriander, salt, and pepper.
2. Form the mixture into two burger patties.
3. Grill or pan-fry the burgers for 4-5 minutes per side or until cooked through.
4. Serve in whole grain burger buns.

Nutritional Information (per serving):
Cal: 520 | Carbs: 22g | Pro: 27g | Fat: 36g
Sugars: 2g | Fiber: 4g

7. Spaghetti Bolognese

Preparation time: 10 minutes
Servings: 2

Ingredients:

- 200g whole wheat spaghetti
- 300g lean ground beef
- 1 cup tomato sauce
- 1 teaspoon dried oregano
- Grated Parmesan cheese for topping

Instructions:

1. Cook whole wheat spaghetti according to package instructions.
2. In a skillet, brown ground beef, then add tomato sauce and dried oregano.
3. Simmer for 5 minutes.
4. Serve Bolognese sauce over cooked whole wheat spaghetti.
5. Top with grated Parmesan cheese.

Nutritional Information (per serving):
Cal: 480 | Carbs: 55g | Pro: 30g | Fat: 14g
Sugars: 7g | Fiber: 9g

8. Moroccan Lamb Tagine with Apricots

Preparation time: 10 minutes
Servings: 2

Ingredients:

- 300g lamb stew meat
- 1 cup dried apricots, halved
- 1 tablespoon Ras el Hanout spice blend
- 1 cup vegetable broth
- Fresh cilantro for garnish

Instructions:

1. In a tagine or a heavy-bottomed pot, brown lamb stew meat.
2. Add dried apricots and Ras el Hanout spice blend.
3. Pour in vegetable broth, cover, and simmer for 15 minutes.
4. Garnish with fresh cilantro before serving.

Nutritional Information (per serving):
Cal: 560 | Carbs: 47g | Pro: 30g | Fat: 29g
Sugars: 32g | Fiber: 7g

9. Greek-Style Beef & Orzo Casserole

Preparation time: 10 minutes
Servings: 2

Ingredients:

- 200g lean ground beef
- 1 cup cooked orzo pasta
- 1 cup tomato sauce
- 1/2 cup crumbled feta cheese
- Fresh oregano for garnish

Instructions:

1. Preheat oven to 375°F (190°C).
2. Brown ground beef in a skillet, then mix with cooked orzo and tomato sauce.
3. Transfer the mixture to a baking dish.
4. Top with crumbled feta cheese.
5. Bake for 20 minutes or until bubbly.
6. Garnish with fresh oregano before serving.

Nutritional Information (per serving):
Cal: 520 | Carbs: 48g | Pro: 28g | Fat: 24g
Sugars: 8g | Fiber: 5g

10. Pork & Vegetable Skewers with Tzatziki

Preparation time: 10 minutes
Servings: 2

Ingredients:

- 300g pork loin, cut into cubes
- 1 zucchini, sliced
- 1 red bell pepper, cut into chunks
- 1/2 cup Tzatziki sauce
- Olive oil for brushing

Instructions:

1. Preheat the grill or a grill pan.
2. Thread pork cubes, zucchini slices, and red bell pepper chunks onto skewers.
3. Brush with olive oil and grill for 5-6 minutes, turning occasionally.
4. Serve with a side of Tzatziki sauce.

Nutritional Information (per serving):
Cal: 480 | Carbs: 20g | Pro: 30g | Fat: 32g
Sugars: 12g | Fiber: 5g

11. Mediterranean Stuffed Cabbage Rolls

Preparation time: 10 minutes
Servings: 2

Ingredients:

- 4 large cabbage leaves, blanched
- 1 cup cooked quinoa
- 1 cup canned chickpeas, drained and rinsed
- 1 cup diced tomatoes (canned or fresh)
- 1 teaspoon Mediterranean herb blend (oregano, thyme, rosemary)
- Salt and pepper to taste

Instructions:

1. Preheat the oven to 375°F (190°C).
2. In a bowl, mix together the cooked quinoa, chickpeas, diced tomatoes, and Mediterranean herb blend.
3. Place a cabbage leaf on a clean surface and spoon 1/4 of the mixture onto the center.
4. Fold the sides of the cabbage leaf over the filling, then roll from the bottom to create a neat roll.
5. Repeat for the remaining cabbage leaves.
6. Place the cabbage rolls in a baking dish, seam side down.
7. Bake in the preheated oven for 10 minutes or until heated through.
8. Season with salt and pepper to taste before serving.

Nutritional Information (per serving):
Cal: 330 | Carbs: 63g | Pro: 15g | Fat: 4g
Sugars: 8g | Fiber: 15g

12. Italian Sausage & White Bean Stew

Preparation time: 10 minutes
Servings: 2

Ingredients:

- 1/2 lb (225g) Italian sausage, sliced
- 1 can (15 oz) white beans, drained and rinsed
- 1 cup diced tomatoes (canned or fresh)
- 1 teaspoon Italian seasoning
- Salt and pepper to taste

Instructions:

1. In a pan over medium heat, brown the sliced Italian sausage until cooked through.
2. Add the white beans, diced tomatoes, and Italian seasoning to the pan. Stir to combine.
3. Simmer for 5 minutes until the stew is heated through.
4. Season with salt and pepper to taste before serving.

Nutritional Information (per serving):
Cal: 490 | Carbs: 42g | Pro: 24g | Fat: 27g
Sugars: 6g | Fiber: 12g

13. Beef and Vegetable Stir-Fry

Preparation time: 10 minutes
Servings: 2

Ingredients:

- 1/2 lb (225g) beef strips
- 2 cups mixed vegetables (bell peppers, zucchini, cherry tomatoes)
- 2 tablespoons olive oil
- 1 teaspoon dried oregano
- Salt and pepper to taste

Instructions:

1. Heat olive oil in a skillet over medium-high heat.
2. Add beef strips and stir-fry until browned.
3. Add mixed vegetables to the skillet and continue stir-frying until vegetables are tender-crisp.
4. Sprinkle dried oregano over the mixture, season with salt and pepper, and toss to combine.
5. Cook for an additional 2 minutes, ensuring the beef is cooked to your liking.
6. Serve immediately.

Nutritional Information (per serving):
Cal: 430 | Carbs: 12g | Pro: 28g | Fat: 32g

Sugars: 6g | Fiber: 4g

14. Baked Greek Meatballs (Keftedes)

Preparation time: 10 minutes
Servings: 2

Ingredients:

- 1/2 lb (225g) ground beef or lamb
- 1/4 cup breadcrumbs
- 1 teaspoon dried oregano
- 1/4 cup grated feta cheese
- Salt and pepper to taste

Instructions:

1. Preheat the oven to 375°F (190°C).
2. In a bowl, combine ground meat, breadcrumbs, oregano, feta, salt, and pepper.
3. Shape the mixture into small meatballs and place them on a baking sheet.
4. Bake for 10 minutes or until meatballs are cooked through and golden.
5. Serve with a side of Greek yogurt or tzatziki.

Nutritional Information (per serving):
Cal: 390 | Carbs: 12g | Pro: 28g | Fat: 26g
Sugars: 2g | Fiber: 1g

15. Pork and Chickpea Stew

Preparation time: 10 minutes
Servings: 2

Ingredients:

- 1/2 lb (225g) pork loin, cubed
- 1 can (15 oz) chickpeas, drained and rinsed
- 1 cup diced tomatoes (canned or fresh)
- 1 teaspoon smoked paprika
- Salt and pepper to taste

Instructions:

1. In a pot over medium heat, brown the pork cubes until cooked through.
2. Add chickpeas, diced tomatoes, and smoked paprika to the pot. Stir to combine.
3. Simmer for 5 minutes until the stew is heated through.
4. Season with salt and pepper to taste before serving.

16. Eggplant and Lamb Moussaka

Preparation time: 10 minutes
Servings: 2

Ingredients:

- 1/2 lb (225g) ground lamb
- 1 large eggplant, sliced
- 1 cup tomato sauce
- 1/2 cup grated Parmesan cheese
- Salt and pepper to taste

Instructions:

1. Preheat the oven to 375°F (190°C).
2. In a skillet over medium heat, brown the ground lamb until cooked through.
3. Layer the sliced eggplant in a baking dish, alternating with the cooked lamb.
4. Pour tomato sauce over the layers and sprinkle Parmesan cheese on top.
5. Bake for 10 minutes or until the cheese is melted and bubbly.
6. Season with salt and pepper to taste before serving.

Nutritional Information (per serving):
Cal: 380 | Carbs: 16g | Pro: 25g | Fat: 25g
Sugars: 10g | Fiber: 7g

17. Mediterranean Beef Skewers

Preparation time: 10 minutes
Servings: 2

Ingredients:

- 1/2 lb (225g) beef sirloin, cubed
- 1 cup cherry tomatoes
- 1/2 cup fresh parsley, chopped
- 2 tablespoons olive oil
- Salt and pepper to taste

Instructions:

1. Thread beef cubes and cherry tomatoes onto skewers.
2. In a bowl, mix chopped parsley with olive oil, salt, and pepper to create chimichurri sauce.

3. Grill or broil the skewers for 5 minutes, turning occasionally, until beef is cooked to your liking.
4. Drizzle chimichurri sauce over the skewers before serving.

Nutritional Information (per serving):
Cal: 420 | Carbs: 8g | Pro: 25g | Fat: 34g
Sugars: 4g | Fiber: 3g

18. Lemon Garlic Marinated Grilled Steak

Preparation time: 10 minutes
Servings: 2

Ingredients:

- 1/2 lb (225g) beef steak (e.g., sirloin, ribeye)
- 2 tablespoons olive oil
- 2 cloves garlic, minced
- Zest and juice of 1 lemon
- Salt and pepper to taste

Instructions:

1. Preheat the grill or grill pan over medium-high heat.
2. In a bowl, whisk together olive oil, minced garlic, lemon zest, lemon juice, salt, and pepper.
3. Marinate the steak in the mixture for 5 minutes.
4. Grill the steak for 3-4 minutes per side or until cooked to your liking.
5. Let the steak rest for a few minutes before slicing.

Nutritional Information (per serving):
Cal: 370 | Carbs: 2g | Pro: 25g | Fat: 30g
Sugars: 1g | Fiber: 0g

19. Greek Lamb and Orzo Soup

Preparation time: 10 minutes
Servings: 2

Ingredients:

- 1/2 lb (225g) lamb stew meat, cubed
- 1/2 cup orzo pasta
- 4 cups chicken broth
- 1 teaspoon dried oregano
- Salt and pepper to taste

Instructions:

1. In a pot, bring chicken broth to a simmer over medium heat.
2. Add lamb cubes and orzo pasta to the pot.
3. Simmer for 8 minutes or until lamb is cooked through and orzo is tender.
4. Season with dried oregano, salt, and pepper before serving.

Nutritional Information (per serving):
Cal: 430 | Carbs: 34g | Pro: 26g | Fat: 20g
Sugars: 0g | Fiber: 2g

20. Pork Chops Sauce

Preparation time: 10 minutes
Servings: 2

Ingredients:

- 2 pork chops
- 1 cup cherry tomatoes, halved
- 1/4 cup Kalamata olives, sliced
- 2 tablespoons olive oil
- Salt and pepper to taste

Instructions:

1. Season pork chops with salt and pepper.
2. In a skillet over medium-high heat, sear the pork chops in olive oil for 3-4 minutes per side or until cooked through.
3. Add cherry tomatoes and olives to the skillet, sauté for an additional 2 minutes.
4. Serve the pork chops topped with the tomato and olive sauce.

Nutritional Information (per serving):
Cal: 480 | Carbs: 6g | Pro: 36g | Fat: 34g
Sugars: 2g | Fiber: 2g

Side Dishes

1. Quinoa Tabbouleh Salad

Preparation time: 10 minutes
Servings: 2

Ingredients:

- 1 cup cooked quinoa, cooled
- 1 cup cherry tomatoes, halved
- 1 cucumber, diced
- 1/4 cup fresh parsley, chopped
- 2 tablespoons extra virgin olive oil
- Salt and pepper to taste

Instructions:

1. In a large bowl, combine the cooked quinoa, cherry tomatoes, cucumber, and fresh parsley.
2. Drizzle the extra virgin olive oil over the ingredients.
3. Season with salt and pepper to taste.
4. Toss the salad gently to combine all the ingredients.
5. Serve immediately or refrigerate until ready to serve.

Nutritional Information (per serving):
Cal: 285 | Carbs: 31g | Pro: 5g | Fat: 16g
Sugars: 3g | Fiber: 5g

2. Roasted Mediterranean Vegetables

Preparation time: 10 minutes
Servings: 2

Ingredients:

- 1 zucchini, sliced
- 1 red bell pepper, sliced
- 1 yellow bell pepper, sliced
- 1 red onion, sliced
- 2 tablespoons olive oil
- Salt and pepper to taste

Instructions:

1. Preheat the oven to 400°F (200°C).
2. Place the sliced zucchini, red bell pepper, yellow bell pepper, and red onion on a baking sheet.
3. Drizzle olive oil over the vegetables and toss to coat evenly.
4. Season with salt and pepper to taste.
5. Roast in the preheated oven for 10 minutes or until the vegetables are tender.

Nutritional Information (per serving):
Cal: 160 | Carbs: 18g | Pro: 2g | Fat: 10g
Sugars: 8g | Fiber: 5g

3. Lemon Garlic Roasted Potatoes

Preparation time: 10 minutes
Servings: 2

Ingredients:

- 2 medium-sized potatoes, diced
- 2 tablespoons olive oil
- 2 cloves garlic, minced
- Juice of 1 lemon
- Salt and pepper to taste

Instructions:

1. Preheat the oven to 425°F (220°C).
2. In a bowl, toss the diced potatoes with olive oil, minced garlic, and lemon juice.
3. Season with salt and pepper to taste.
4. Spread the potatoes on a baking sheet in a single layer.
5. Roast in the preheated oven for 10 minutes or until golden brown and crispy.

Nutritional Information (per serving):
Cal: 245 | Carbs: 32g | Pro: 3g | Fat: 12g
Sugars: 2g | Fiber: 4g

4. Greek-Style Roasted Brussels Sprouts

Preparation time: 10 minutes
Servings: 2

Ingredients:

- 2 cups Brussels sprouts, halved
- 2 tablespoons olive oil
- 1 teaspoon dried oregano
- Salt and pepper to taste
- 2 tablespoons feta cheese, crumbled (optional)

Instructions:

1. Preheat the oven to 400°F (200°C).
2. Toss the Brussels sprouts with olive oil, dried oregano, salt, and pepper.
3. Spread the Brussels sprouts on a baking sheet.

4. Roast in the preheated oven for 10 minutes or until they are golden brown and crispy.
5. Optional: Sprinkle crumbled feta cheese over the roasted Brussels sprouts before serving.

Nutritional Information (per serving):
Cal: 130 | Carbs: 12g | Pro: 4g | Fat: 9g
Sugars: 2g | Fiber: 5g

5. Tomato & Cucumber Salad with Feta

Preparation time: 10 minutes
Servings: 2

Ingredients:

- 1 cup cherry tomatoes, halved
- 1 cucumber, diced
- 2 tablespoons red onion, finely chopped
- 2 tablespoons feta cheese, crumbled
- 1 tablespoon extra virgin olive oil
- Salt and pepper to taste

Instructions:

1. In a bowl, combine the cherry tomatoes, cucumber, red onion, and crumbled feta cheese.
2. Drizzle the extra virgin olive oil over the salad.
3. Season with salt and pepper to taste.
4. Toss gently to combine all the ingredients.
5. Serve immediately.

Nutritional Information (per serving):
Cal: 95 | Carbs: 6g | Pro: 3g | Fat: 7g
Sugars: 3g | Fiber: 2g

6. Mediterranean Couscous

Preparation time: 10 minutes
Servings: 2

Ingredients:

- 1 cup couscous, cooked
- 2 tablespoons pine nuts, toasted
- 2 tablespoons fresh parsley, chopped
- 1 tablespoon extra virgin olive oil
- Salt and pepper to taste

Instructions:

1. In a bowl, fluff the cooked couscous with a fork.

2. Add toasted pine nuts and fresh parsley to the couscous.
3. Drizzle with extra virgin olive oil.
4. Season with salt and pepper to taste.
5. Toss gently to combine all the ingredients.

Nutritional Information (per serving):
Cal: 315 | Carbs: 56g | Pro: 9g | Fat: 6g
Sugars: 1g | Fiber: 4g

7. Grilled Asparagus

Preparation time: 10 minutes
Servings: 2

Ingredients:

- 1 bunch asparagus, trimmed
- 1 tablespoon olive oil
- Zest of 1 lemon
- 2 tablespoons Parmesan cheese, grated
- Salt and pepper to taste

Instructions:

1. Preheat the grill or grill pan over medium-high heat.
2. Toss asparagus with olive oil, lemon zest, salt, and pepper.
3. Grill the asparagus for 3-4 minutes, turning occasionally, until tender.
4. Sprinkle grated Parmesan cheese over the grilled asparagus before serving.

Nutritional Information (per serving):
Cal: 80 | Carbs: 5g | Pro: 4g | Fat: 6g
Sugars: 2g | Fiber: 2g

8. Caprese Quinoa Salad

Preparation time: 10 minutes
Servings: 2

Ingredients:

- 1 cup cooked quinoa, cooled
- 1 cup cherry tomatoes, halved
- 1/2 cup fresh mozzarella balls
- 2 tablespoons fresh basil, chopped
- 1 tablespoon balsamic glaze
- Salt and pepper to taste

Instructions:

1. In a bowl, combine cooked quinoa, cherry tomatoes, fresh mozzarella balls, and fresh basil.
2. Drizzle with balsamic glaze.
3. Season with salt and pepper to taste.
4. Toss gently to combine all the ingredients.
5. Serve immediately.

Nutritional Information (per serving):
Cal: 295 | Carbs: 32g | Pro: 11g | Fat: 14g
Sugars: 3g | Fiber: 4g

9. Baked Zucchini Fritters

Preparation time: 10 minutes
Servings: 2

Ingredients:

- 2 medium-sized zucchinis, grated
- 1/4 cup breadcrumbs
- 1 egg, beaten
- 1 tablespoon olive oil
- Salt and pepper to taste

Instructions:

1. Preheat the oven to 425°F (220°C).
2. In a bowl, combine grated zucchini, breadcrumbs, beaten egg, salt, and pepper.
3. Form the mixture into small patties and place on a baking sheet.
4. Drizzle olive oil over the fritters.
5. Bake in the preheated oven for 10 minutes or until golden brown and cooked through.

Nutritional Information (per serving):
Cal: 160 | Carbs: 18g | Pro: 6g | Fat: 8g
Sugars: 5g | Fiber: 3g

10. Roasted Sweet Potatoes

Preparation time: 10 minutes
Servings: 2

Ingredients:

- 2 medium-sized sweet potatoes, peeled and diced
- 2 tablespoons olive oil
- 2 tablespoons tahini
- 1 tablespoon honey
- Salt and pepper to taste

Instructions:

1. Preheat the oven to 425°F (220°C).
2. Toss the diced sweet potatoes with olive oil, salt, and pepper.
3. Spread the sweet potatoes on a baking sheet in a single layer.
4. Roast in the preheated oven for 10 minutes or until they are tender.
5. In a small bowl, mix tahini and honey to create the drizzle.
6. Drizzle the tahini mixture over the roasted sweet potatoes before serving.

Nutritional Information (per serving):
Cal: 250 | Carbs: 30g | Pro: 3g | Fat: 14g
Sugars: 10g | Fiber: 4g

11. Orzo Pasta with Vegetables

Preparation time: 5 minutes
Servings: 2

Ingredients:

- 1 cup orzo pasta
- 1 cup cherry tomatoes, halved
- 1/2 cup cucumber, diced
- 1/4 cup Kalamata olives, sliced
- 2 tablespoons feta cheese, crumbled

Instructions:

1. Cook orzo pasta according to package instructions. Drain and set aside.
2. In a bowl, combine cooked orzo, cherry tomatoes, cucumber, Kalamata olives, and feta cheese.
3. Toss gently to combine.
4. Serve immediately, and enjoy this quick and refreshing Mediterranean pasta dish!

Nutritional Information (per serving):
Cal: 370 | Carbs: 65g | Pro: 12g | Fat: 6g
Sugars: 4g | Fiber: 4g

12. Greek-Style Roasted Cauliflower

Preparation time: 5 minutes
Servings: 2

Ingredients:

- 1 small cauliflower, cut into florets

- 2 tablespoons olive oil
- 1 teaspoon dried oregano
- Salt and pepper, to taste

Instructions:

1. Preheat the oven to 425°F (220°C).
2. In a bowl, toss cauliflower florets with olive oil, dried oregano, salt, and pepper.
3. Spread the cauliflower on a baking sheet in a single layer.
4. Roast for 10 minutes or until golden and tender.
5. Serve hot, and savor the Greek-inspired flavors of this simple roasted cauliflower!

Nutritional Information (per serving):
Cal: 120 | Carbs: 10g | Pro: 4g | Fat: 8g
Sugars: 4g | Fiber: 4g

13. Spinach & Feta Stuffed Mushrooms

Preparation time: 10 minutes
Servings: 2

Ingredients:

- 8 large mushrooms, cleaned and stems removed
- 1 cup fresh spinach, chopped
- 1/2 cup feta cheese, crumbled
- Salt and pepper, to taste

Instructions:

1. Preheat the oven to 375°F (190°C).
2. In a bowl, mix chopped spinach, feta cheese, salt, and pepper.
3. Stuff each mushroom cap with the spinach and feta mixture.
4. Place the stuffed mushrooms on a baking sheet.
5. Bake for 8-10 minutes or until mushrooms are tender.
6. Serve warm, and enjoy these delightful spinach and feta stuffed mushrooms!

Nutritional Information (per serving):
Cal: 85 | Carbs: 4g | Pro: 6g | Fat: 5g
Sugars: 2g | Fiber: 1g

14. Lemon Herb Quinoa Pilaf

Preparation time: 10 minutes

Servings: 2

Ingredients:

- 1 cup cooked quinoa
- 1 tablespoon olive oil
- 1 tablespoon fresh lemon juice
- 1 teaspoon dried mixed herbs (rosemary, thyme, oregano)
- Salt and pepper, to taste

Instructions:

1. In a bowl, combine cooked quinoa, olive oil, fresh lemon juice, dried herbs, salt, and pepper.
2. Toss gently until well combined.
3. Adjust seasoning to taste.
4. Serve as a side dish or a light main course, and relish the zesty flavors of this lemon herb quinoa pilaf!

Nutritional Information (per serving):
Cal: 240 | Carbs: 28g | Pro: 4g | Fat: 12g
Sugars: 1g | Fiber: 3g

15. Olive Oil & Herb Marinated Artichokes

Preparation time: 5 minutes
Servings: 2

Ingredients:

- 1 cup artichoke hearts (canned or marinated)
- 2 tablespoons extra virgin olive oil
- 1 teaspoon dried Italian herbs
- Salt and pepper, to taste

Instructions:

1. Drain artichoke hearts and place them in a bowl.
2. Drizzle with extra virgin olive oil.
3. Sprinkle with dried Italian herbs, salt, and pepper.
4. Toss gently to coat the artichokes in the marinade.
5. Allow the flavors to meld for a few minutes before serving.
6. Enjoy these marinated artichokes as a flavorful and easy appetizer!

Nutritional Information (per serving):
Cal: 160 | Carbs: 7g | Pro: 2g | Fat: 15g

Sugars: 1g | Fiber: 4g

16. Mediterranean Rice Pilaf

Preparation time: 10 minutes
Servings: 2

Ingredients:

- 1 cup cooked brown rice
- 2 tablespoons slivered almonds, toasted
- 1 tablespoon olive oil
- 1 teaspoon dried parsley
- Salt and pepper, to taste

Instructions:

1. In a pan, heat olive oil over medium heat.
2. Add cooked brown rice and toasted slivered almonds.
3. Stir in dried parsley, salt, and pepper.
4. Sauté for 2-3 minutes until heated through.
5. Serve as a side dish, and savor the nutty goodness of this Mediterranean rice pilaf!

Nutritional Information (per serving):
Cal: 240 | Carbs: 35g | Pro: 5g | Fat: 9g
Sugars: 0g | Fiber: 4g

17. Baked Feta with Tomatoes & Olives

Preparation time: 10 minutes
Servings: 2

Ingredients:

- 1 block feta cheese (200g)
- 1 cup cherry tomatoes, halved
- 1/4 cup Kalamata olives, sliced
- 1 tablespoon olive oil
- Fresh oregano for garnish (optional)

Instructions:

1. Preheat the oven to 400°F (200°C).
2. Place the block of feta in the center of a baking dish.
3. Surround the feta with halved cherry tomatoes and sliced Kalamata olives.
4. Drizzle olive oil over the top.
5. Bake for 8-10 minutes or until the feta is soft and tomatoes are juicy.
6. Garnish with fresh oregano if desired.

7. Serve with crusty bread and enjoy this warm and savory baked feta dish!

Nutritional Information (per serving):
Cal: 320 | Carbs: 9g | Pro: 14g | Fat: 26g
Sugars: 5g | Fiber: 2g

18. Grilled Eggplant with Garlic & Herbs

Preparation time: 10 minutes
Servings: 2

Ingredients:

- 1 medium-sized eggplant, sliced
- 2 tablespoons olive oil
- 2 cloves garlic, minced
- 1 teaspoon dried Italian herbs
- Salt and pepper, to taste

Instructions:

1. Preheat a grill or grill pan over medium heat.
2. In a bowl, toss eggplant slices with olive oil, minced garlic, dried Italian herbs, salt, and pepper.
3. Grill the eggplant for 3-4 minutes on each side or until tender and grill marks appear.
4. Serve hot, and relish the smoky flavor of this easy grilled eggplant!

Nutritional Information (per serving):
Cal: 160 | Carbs: 20g | Pro: 3g | Fat: 9g
Sugars: 9g | Fiber: 9g

19. Herbed Farro Salad

Preparation time: 10 minutes
Servings: 2

Ingredients:

- 1 cup cooked farro
- 1 tablespoon fresh lemon juice
- 2 tablespoons olive oil
- 1 tablespoon fresh parsley, chopped
- Salt and pepper, to taste

Instructions:

1. In a bowl, combine cooked farro, fresh lemon juice, olive oil, chopped parsley, salt, and pepper.

2. Toss gently until well combined.
3. Adjust seasoning to taste.
4. Serve as a side dish or a light main course, and enjoy the hearty goodness of this herbed farro salad!

Nutritional Information (per serving):
Cal: 280 | Carbs: 45g | Pro: 6g | Fat: 10g
Sugars: 0g | Fiber: 9g

20. Greek-Style Lentil Salad

Preparation time: 10 minutes
Servings: 2

Ingredients:

- 1 cup cooked green lentils
- 1/2 cup cherry tomatoes, halved
- 1/4 cup red onion, finely chopped
- 2 tablespoons feta cheese, crumbled
- 1 tablespoon extra virgin olive oil

Instructions:

1. In a bowl, combine cooked green lentils, cherry tomatoes, red onion, and feta cheese.
2. Drizzle extra virgin olive oil over the top.
3. Toss gently until well combined.
4. Adjust seasoning to taste.
5. Serve chilled or at room temperature, and savor the delightful flavors of this Greek-style lentil salad!

Nutritional Information (per serving):
Cal: 320 | Carbs: 40g | Pro: 16g | Fat: 12g
Sugars: 5g | Fiber: 16g

Vegetables and Grains

1. Ratatouille with Herbs de Provence

Preparation time: 10 minutes
Servings: 2

Ingredients:

- 1 small eggplant, diced
- 1 zucchini, diced
- 1 red bell pepper, diced
- 1 cup cherry tomatoes, halved
- 1 tablespoon Herbs de Provence
- Salt and pepper to taste

Instructions:

1. In a large skillet over medium heat, add the diced eggplant, zucchini, red bell pepper, and cherry tomatoes.
2. Season with Herbs de Provence, salt, and pepper.
3. Sauté the vegetables for 7-8 minutes or until they are tender but not mushy.
4. Stir occasionally to ensure even cooking.
5. Once cooked, remove from heat and serve immediately.

Nutritional Information (per serving):
Cal: 75 | Carbs: 18g | Pro: 3g | Fat: 0.5g
Sugars: 8g | Fiber: 7g

2. Mediterranean Quinoa Stuffed Bell Peppers

Preparation time: 10 minutes
Servings: 2

Ingredients:

- 1 cup cooked quinoa
- 1 cup cherry tomatoes, diced
- 1/2 cup cucumber, diced
- 1/4 cup feta cheese, crumbled
- 2 large bell peppers, halved and seeds removed

Instructions:

1. In a bowl, mix cooked quinoa, diced cherry tomatoes, cucumber, and crumbled feta cheese.
2. Stuff the halved bell peppers with the quinoa mixture.
3. Serve immediately or refrigerate for a refreshing cold option.

Nutritional Information (per serving):
Cal: 250 | Carbs: 40g | Pro: 10g | Fat: 6g
Sugars: 7g | Fiber: 7g

3. Eggplant Caponata with Crostini

Preparation time: 10 minutes
Servings: 2

Ingredients:

- 1 medium eggplant, diced
- 1/2 cup cherry tomatoes, quartered
- 1/4 cup green olives, sliced
- 2 tablespoons balsamic vinegar
- Whole wheat baguette, sliced and toasted

Instructions:

1. In a skillet over medium heat, sauté the diced eggplant until softened.
2. Add cherry tomatoes, sliced olives, and balsamic vinegar.
3. Cook for an additional 3-4 minutes, stirring occasionally.
4. Serve the eggplant caponata over whole wheat crostini slices.

Nutritional Information (per serving):
Cal: 180 | Carbs: 35g | Pro: 6g | Fat: 3g
Sugars: 12g | Fiber: 10g

4. Bulgur Pilaf with Roasted Vegetables

Preparation time: 10 minutes
Servings: 2

Ingredients:

- 1 cup cooked bulgur
- 1 cup mixed roasted vegetables (e.g., bell peppers, zucchini, cherry tomatoes)
- 1 tablespoon olive oil
- Salt and pepper to taste
- Fresh parsley for garnish

Instructions:

1. In a bowl, mix cooked bulgur with roasted vegetables.
2. Drizzle olive oil over the mixture and season with salt and pepper.
3. Toss until well combined.

4. Garnish with fresh parsley and serve.

Nutritional Information (per serving):
Cal: 220 | Carbs: 38g | Pro: 6g | Fat: 6g
Sugars: 3g | Fiber: 9g

5. Greek Spanakorizo

Preparation time: 10 minutes
Servings: 2

Ingredients:

- 1 cup cooked rice
- 2 cups fresh spinach
- 1 lemon, juiced
- 2 tablespoons olive oil
- Feta cheese for garnish

Instructions:

1. In a skillet over medium heat, sauté fresh spinach until wilted.
2. Add cooked rice to the skillet and stir.
3. Drizzle olive oil and lemon juice over the mixture.
4. Garnish with crumbled feta cheese and serve.

Nutritional Information (per serving):
Cal: 280 | Carbs: 45g | Pro: 5g | Fat: 8g
Sugars: 2g | Fiber: 3g

6. Tomato Basil Risotto

Preparation time: 10 minutes
Servings: 2

Ingredients:

- 1 cup Arborio rice
- 1/2 cup cherry tomatoes, halved
- 2 cups vegetable broth
- 1/4 cup fresh basil, chopped
- 1 tablespoon olive oil

Instructions:

1. In a saucepan, heat olive oil and add Arborio rice. Sauté for 2 minutes.
2. Pour in vegetable broth gradually while stirring continuously.
3. Add cherry tomatoes and continue stirring until the rice is cooked and creamy.

4. Stir in chopped fresh basil and serve immediately.

Nutritional Information (per serving):
Cal: 320 | Carbs: 65g | Pro: 6g | Fat: 5g
Sugars: 2g | Fiber: 2g

7. Lentil and Vegetable Moussaka

Preparation time: 10 minutes
Servings: 2

Ingredients:

- 1 cup cooked lentils
- 1 cup diced eggplant
- 1 cup tomato sauce
- 1/4 cup feta cheese, crumbled
- Fresh parsley for garnish

Instructions:

1. In a baking dish, layer cooked lentils, diced eggplant, and tomato sauce.
2. Top with crumbled feta cheese.
3. Bake in a preheated oven at 350°F (180°C) for 5-7 minutes.
4. Garnish with fresh parsley and serve.

Nutritional Information (per serving):
Cal: 250 | Carbs: 40g | Pro: 15g | Fat: 5g
Sugars: 7g | Fiber: 15g

8. Grilled Portobello Mushrooms

Preparation time: 10 minutes
Servings: 2

Ingredients:

- 2 large Portobello mushrooms
- 2 tablespoons balsamic glaze
- 1 tablespoon olive oil
- Salt and pepper to taste
- Fresh thyme for garnish

Instructions:

1. Preheat the grill or grill pan over medium-high heat.
2. Brush Portobello mushrooms with olive oil and season with salt and pepper.
3. Grill for 4-5 minutes on each side.

4. Drizzle balsamic glaze over the grilled mushrooms.
5. Garnish with fresh thyme and serve.

Nutritional Information (per serving):
Cal: 120 | Carbs: 15g | Pro: 5g | Fat: 6g
Sugars: 7g | Fiber: 3g

9. Mediterranean Chickpea & Vegetable

Preparation time: 10 minutes
Servings: 2

Ingredients:

- 1 can (15 oz) chickpeas, drained and rinsed
- 1 cup mixed stir-fry vegetables (bell peppers, broccoli, carrots)
- 2 tablespoons olive oil
- 1 teaspoon dried oregano
- Lemon wedges for serving

Instructions:

1. In a wok or skillet, heat olive oil over medium-high heat.
2. Add chickpeas and stir-fry vegetables. Cook for 5-7 minutes.
3. Sprinkle dried oregano over the mixture and toss.
4. Serve with lemon wedges on the side.

Nutritional Information (per serving):
Cal: 320 | Carbs: 45g | Pro: 11g | Fat: 12g
Sugars: 8g | Fiber: 12g

10. Farro and Roasted Vegetable Bowl

Preparation time: 10 minutes
Servings: 2

Ingredients:

- 1 cup cooked farro
- 1 cup mixed roasted vegetables (sweet potatoes, Brussels sprouts, cherry tomatoes)
- 2 tablespoons tahini
- 1 tablespoon lemon juice
- Chopped cilantro for garnish

Instructions:

1. In a bowl, arrange cooked farro and mixed roasted vegetables.

2. In a small bowl, mix tahini and lemon juice to create a dressing.
3. Drizzle the tahini dressing over the Buddha bowl.
4. Garnish with chopped cilantro and serve.

Nutritional Information (per serving):
Cal: 350 | Carbs: 58g | Pro: 10g | Fat: 10g
Sugars: 4g | Fiber: 11g

11. Stuffed Tomatoes

Preparation time: 10 minutes
Servings: 2

Ingredients:

- 2 large tomatoes
- 1/2 cup fine bulgur
- 2 tablespoons pine nuts
- 1 tablespoon olive oil
- Salt and pepper to taste

Instructions:

1. Cut the tops off the tomatoes and scoop out the seeds and pulp, leaving a shell. Sprinkle the inside of the tomatoes with a pinch of salt.
2. In a bowl, combine the bulgur with enough hot water to cover it. Let it sit for 5 minutes until it absorbs the water and becomes tender.
3. Toast the pine nuts in a dry skillet over medium heat until golden brown.
4. Fluff the bulgur with a fork and mix in the toasted pine nuts. Season with salt and pepper to taste.
5. Stuff the tomatoes with the bulgur and pine nut mixture, pressing down gently to pack it.
6. Drizzle olive oil over the top and serve immediately.

Nutritional Information (per serving):
Cal: 236 | Carbs: 34g | Pro: 6g | Fat: 9g
Sugars: 4g | Fiber: 8g

12. Spaghetti Aglio e Olio

Preparation time: 10 minutes
Servings: 2

Ingredients:

- 200g spaghetti
- 4 cloves garlic, thinly sliced
- 1/4 cup olive oil
- 1 cup cherry tomatoes, halved
- Salt and red pepper flakes to taste

Instructions:

1. Cook the spaghetti according to package instructions. Reserve 1/4 cup of pasta water before draining.
2. In a large skillet, heat olive oil over medium heat. Add sliced garlic and cook until golden but not burnt.
3. Add cherry tomatoes to the skillet, sauté for 2-3 minutes until they begin to soften.
4. Toss in the cooked spaghetti, adding reserved pasta water as needed to create a light sauce. Season with salt and red pepper flakes.
5. Serve immediately, drizzling with extra olive oil if desired.

Nutritional Information (per serving):
Cal: 430 | Carbs: 56g | Pro: 9g | Fat: 19g
Sugars: 3g | Fiber: 3g

13. Lemon Herb Quinoa

Preparation time: 10 minutes
Servings: 2

Ingredients:

- 1 cup quinoa, cooked
- 1 cup mixed grilled vegetables (zucchini, bell peppers, cherry tomatoes)
- Zest and juice of 1 lemon
- 2 tablespoons fresh herbs (parsley, mint, or basil), chopped
- Salt and pepper to taste

Instructions:

1. In a bowl, combine cooked quinoa, grilled vegetables, lemon zest, and lemon juice.
2. Add fresh herbs and toss everything together. Season with salt and pepper to taste.
3. Serve immediately as a light and refreshing side dish.

Nutritional Information (per serving):
Cal: 320 | Carbs: 58g | Pro: 10g | Fat: 5g
Sugars: 3g | Fiber: 7g

14. Greek-Style Casserole

Preparation time: 10 minutes
Servings: 2

Ingredients:

- 1 large eggplant, sliced
- 1/2 cup cooked green lentils
- 1 cup tomato sauce
- 1/2 cup feta cheese, crumbled
- Olive oil for drizzling

Instructions:

1. Preheat the oven to 400°F (200°C).
2. In a baking dish, layer the sliced eggplant, cooked green lentils, and tomato sauce.
3. Sprinkle crumbled feta cheese over the top and drizzle with olive oil.
4. Bake for 20-25 minutes or until the eggplant is tender and the top is golden.
5. Serve hot as a comforting and nutritious main dish.

Nutritional Information (per serving):
Cal: 380 | Carbs: 40g | Pro: 16g | Fat: 18g
Sugars: 12g | Fiber: 15g

15. Mediterranean Zucchini Noodles

Preparation time: 10 minutes
Servings: 2

Ingredients:

- 2 medium zucchinis, spiralized
- 1/2 cup cherry tomatoes, halved
- 3 tablespoons store-bought pesto
- 1/4 cup feta cheese, crumbled
- Salt and pepper to taste

Instructions:

1. Spiralize the zucchinis to create noodles.
2. In a pan over medium heat, sauté zucchini noodles until just tender.
3. Toss in cherry tomatoes and cook for an additional 2 minutes.
4. Stir in pesto, ensuring even coating of noodles.
5. Top with crumbled feta, season with salt and pepper, and serve.

Nutritional Information (per serving):
Cal: 220 | Carbs: 12g | Pro: 6g | Fat: 17g
Sugars: 6g | Fiber: 4g

16. Roasted Vegetable & Pearl Couscous Salad

Preparation time: 10 minutes
Servings: 2

Ingredients:

- 1 cup pearl couscous, cooked
- 1 cup mixed roasted vegetables (bell peppers, cherry tomatoes, red onion)
- 2 tablespoons olive oil
- 1 tablespoon balsamic vinegar
- Salt and pepper to taste

Instructions:

1. In a bowl, combine cooked pearl couscous and mixed roasted vegetables.
2. Drizzle olive oil and balsamic vinegar over the mixture, tossing to coat.
3. Season with salt and pepper to taste.
4. Serve as a hearty and flavorful salad.

Nutritional Information (per serving):
Cal: 340 | Carbs: 50g | Pro: 7g | Fat: 12g
Sugars: 4g | Fiber: 6g

17. Baked Greek Orzo with Feta & Olives

Preparation time: 10 minutes
Servings: 2

Ingredients:

- 1 cup orzo, cooked
- 1/2 cup crumbled feta cheese
- 1/4 cup Kalamata olives, sliced
- 2 tablespoons olive oil
- Fresh oregano for garnish

Instructions:

1. Preheat the oven to 375°F (190°C).
2. In a baking dish, combine cooked orzo, crumbled feta, and sliced Kalamata olives.
3. Drizzle olive oil over the mixture and toss to combine.
4. Bake for 10 minutes or until the feta is slightly melted.

5. Garnish with fresh oregano before serving.

Nutritional Information (per serving):
Cal: 420 | Carbs: 52g | Pro: 11g | Fat: 19g
Sugars: 2g | Fiber: 3g

18. Spinach & Feta Stuffed Acorn Squash

Preparation time: 10 minutes
Servings: 2

Ingredients:

- 1 acorn squash, halved and seeds removed
- 2 cups fresh spinach, chopped
- 1/2 cup crumbled feta cheese
- 2 tablespoons olive oil
- Salt and pepper to taste

Instructions:

1. Preheat the oven to 375°F (190°C).
2. Place acorn squash halves on a baking sheet.
3. In a bowl, mix chopped spinach and crumbled feta. Stuff the squash halves with the mixture.
4. Drizzle olive oil over the top and season with salt and pepper.
5. Bake for 30-35 minutes or until the squash is fork-tender.

Nutritional Information (per serving):
Cal: 280 | Carbs: 32g | Pro: 7g | Fat: 16g
Sugars: 2g | Fiber: 6g

19. Barley and Vegetable Pilaf

Preparation time: 10 minutes
Servings: 2

Ingredients:

- 1/2 cup barley, cooked
- 1 cup mixed vegetables (carrots, peas, corn)
- 1 tablespoon olive oil
- 2 tablespoons chopped fresh parsley
- Lemon wedges for serving

Instructions:

1. In a pan, sauté mixed vegetables in olive oil until tender.

2. Add cooked barley to the pan and toss until well combined.
3. Stir in chopped fresh parsley and cook for an additional 2 minutes.
4. Serve with lemon wedges for a burst of citrus flavor.

Nutritional Information (per serving):
Cal: 280 | Carbs: 50g | Pro: 8g | Fat: 6g
Sugars: 4g | Fiber: 10g

20. Mediterranean Ratatouille Pasta

Preparation time: 10 minutes
Servings: 2

Ingredients:

- 200g whole wheat spaghetti
- 1 cup ratatouille (mixed sautéed vegetables, like eggplant, zucchini, bell peppers, tomatoes)
- 2 tablespoons olive oil
- 1/4 cup grated Parmesan cheese
- Fresh basil for garnish

Instructions:

1. Cook whole wheat spaghetti according to package instructions.
2. In a pan, heat olive oil and add ratatouille, sautéing until heated through.
3. Toss the cooked pasta with the ratatouille mixture.
4. Serve topped with grated Parmesan cheese and fresh basil.

Nutritional Information (per serving):
Cal: 380 | Carbs: 54g | Pro: 14g | Fat: 13g
Sugars: 6g | Fiber: 10g

Salads

1. Greek Salad with Feta & Kalamata Olives

Preparation time: 10 minutes
Servings: 2

Ingredients:

- 2 cups cherry tomatoes, halved
- 1 cucumber, diced
- 1/2 cup feta cheese, crumbled
- 1/4 cup Kalamata olives, pitted and sliced
- 2 tablespoons extra-virgin olive oil
- Salt and pepper, to taste

Instructions:

1. In a large bowl, combine the cherry tomatoes, cucumber, feta cheese, and Kalamata olives.
2. Drizzle the extra-virgin olive oil over the salad.
3. Season with salt and pepper to taste.
4. Toss gently to combine all the ingredients.
5. Serve immediately and enjoy the refreshing flavors of this classic Greek salad.

Nutritional Information (per serving):
Cal: 210 | Carbs: 10g | Pro: 6g | Fat: 18g
Sugars: 5g | Fiber: 3g

2. Caprese Salad with Balsamic Glaze

Preparation time: 10 minutes
Servings: 2

Ingredients:

- 2 large tomatoes, sliced
- 1 ball fresh mozzarella, sliced
- 1/4 cup fresh basil leaves
- 2 tablespoons balsamic glaze
- Salt and pepper, to taste

Instructions:

1. Arrange alternating slices of tomatoes and fresh mozzarella on a serving plate.
2. Tuck fresh basil leaves between the tomato and mozzarella slices.
3. Drizzle balsamic glaze over the salad.
4. Season with salt and pepper to taste.
5. Serve immediately, and savor the simplicity of this delightful Caprese salad.

Nutritional Information (per serving):

Cal: 190 | Carbs: 10g | Pro: 12g | Fat: 12g
Sugars: 5g | Fiber: 2g

3. Mediterranean Chickpea Salad

Preparation time: 10 minutes
Servings: 2

Ingredients:

- 1 can (15 oz) chickpeas, drained and rinsed
- 1 cup cherry tomatoes, halved
- 1/2 cucumber, diced
- 2 tablespoons red onion, finely chopped
- 2 tablespoons extra-virgin olive oil
- Salt and pepper, to taste

Instructions:

1. In a bowl, combine chickpeas, cherry tomatoes, cucumber, and red onion.
2. Drizzle extra-virgin olive oil over the salad.
3. Season with salt and pepper to taste.
4. Toss gently until well combined.
5. Serve immediately, and enjoy the vibrant flavors of this Mediterranean chickpea salad.

Nutritional Information (per serving):
Cal: 280 | Carbs: 32g | Pro: 10g | Fat: 14g
Sugars: 7g | Fiber: 9g

4. Tuna and White Bean Salad

Preparation time: 10 minutes
Servings: 2

Ingredients:

- 1 can (5 oz) tuna, drained
- 1 can (15 oz) white beans, drained and rinsed
- 1/4 cup red onion, finely chopped
- 2 tablespoons lemon juice
- 2 tablespoons fresh parsley, chopped

Instructions:

1. In a bowl, combine tuna, white beans, red onion, lemon juice, and fresh parsley.
2. Toss gently until all ingredients are well mixed.
3. Serve immediately, and enjoy the protein-packed goodness of this tuna and white bean salad.

Nutritional Information (per serving):
Cal: 320 | Carbs: 38g | Pro: 28g | Fat: 6g
Sugars: 2g | Fiber: 12g

5. Watermelon & Feta Salad with Mint

Preparation time: 10 minutes
Servings: 2

Ingredients:

- 2 cups watermelon, cubed
- 1/2 cup feta cheese, crumbled
- Fresh mint leaves, for garnish
- 1 tablespoon balsamic glaze
- Salt, to taste

Instructions:

1. Arrange watermelon cubes on a serving plate.
2. Sprinkle crumbled feta over the watermelon.
3. Garnish with fresh mint leaves.
4. Drizzle balsamic glaze over the salad.
5. Sprinkle a pinch of salt to enhance flavors.
6. Serve immediately and enjoy the sweet and savory combination.

Nutritional Information (per serving):
Cal: 170 | Carbs: 20g | Pro: 6g | Fat: 8g
Sugars: 15g | Fiber: 1g

6. Quinoa and Avocado Salad

Preparation time: 10 minutes
Servings: 2

Ingredients:

- 1 cup cooked quinoa
- 1 avocado, diced
- 1/4 cup cherry tomatoes, halved
- 2 tablespoons fresh lemon juice
- 1 tablespoon extra-virgin olive oil

Instructions:

1. In a bowl, combine cooked quinoa, diced avocado, and cherry tomatoes.
2. In a small bowl, whisk together fresh lemon juice and extra-virgin olive oil to create the vinaigrette.
3. Drizzle the lemon vinaigrette over the salad.

4. Toss gently until all ingredients are well coated.
5. Serve immediately, and relish the wholesome goodness of this quinoa and avocado salad.

Nutritional Information (per serving):
Cal: 330 | Carbs: 33g | Pro: 7g | Fat: 21g
Sugars: 2g | Fiber: 8g

7. Tabouleh Salad with Parsley & Tomatoes

Preparation time: 10 minutes
Servings: 2

Ingredients:

- 1 cup fresh parsley, finely chopped
- 1 cup cherry tomatoes, diced
- 1/4 cup red onion, finely chopped
- 2 tablespoons fresh lemon juice
- 2 tablespoons extra-virgin olive oil

Instructions:

1. In a bowl, combine chopped parsley, diced cherry tomatoes, and finely chopped red onion.
2. In a small bowl, whisk together fresh lemon juice and extra-virgin olive oil to create the dressing.
3. Drizzle the dressing over the salad.
4. Toss gently until all ingredients are well combined.
5. Serve immediately, and enjoy the zesty flavors of this tabouleh salad.

Nutritional Information (per serving):
Cal: 120 | Carbs: 8g | Pro: 2g | Fat: 10g
Sugars: 2g | Fiber: 2g

8. Italian Panzanella Bread Salad

Preparation time: 10 minutes
Servings: 2

Ingredients:

- 2 cups day-old crusty bread, cubed
- 1 cup cherry tomatoes, halved
- 1/2 cucumber, diced
- 2 tablespoons red wine vinegar
- 2 tablespoons extra-virgin olive oil

Instructions:

1. In a large bowl, combine cubed bread, cherry tomatoes, and diced cucumber.
2. In a small bowl, whisk together red wine vinegar and extra-virgin olive oil to create the dressing.
3. Drizzle the dressing over the salad.
4. Toss gently until the bread absorbs the dressing and the ingredients are well mixed.
5. Serve immediately, and savor the delightful crunch of this Italian panzanella bread salad.

Nutritional Information (per serving):
Cal: 290 | Carbs: 31g | Pro: 5g | Fat: 16g
Sugars: 4g | Fiber: 3g

9. Mediterranean Lentil Salad

Preparation time: 10 minutes
Servings: 2

Ingredients:

- 1 cup cooked green lentils
- 1/2 cup cherry tomatoes, halved
- 1/4 cup red onion, finely chopped
- 2 tablespoons feta cheese, crumbled
- 2 tablespoons balsamic vinaigrette

Instructions:

1. In a bowl, combine cooked green lentils, cherry tomatoes, finely chopped red onion, and crumbled feta cheese.
2. Drizzle balsamic vinaigrette over the salad.
3. Toss gently until all ingredients are well coated.
4. Serve immediately and enjoy the protein-packed goodness of this Mediterranean lentil salad.

Nutritional Information (per serving):
Cal: 280 | Carbs: 38g | Pro: 16g | Fat: 8g
Sugars: 5g | Fiber: 16g

10. Roasted Beet and Goat Cheese

Preparation time: 10 minutes
Servings: 2

Ingredients:

- 2 medium-sized beets, roasted and diced
- 2 cups mixed salad greens
- 2 tablespoons goat cheese, crumbled
- 2 tablespoons balsamic vinaigrette
- Salt and pepper, to taste

Instructions:

1. In a bowl, combine diced roasted beets and mixed salad greens.
2. Sprinkle crumbled goat cheese over the salad.
3. Drizzle balsamic vinaigrette over the ingredients.
4. Season with salt and pepper to taste.
5. Toss gently until all components are well mixed.
6. Serve immediately and relish the earthy flavors of this roasted beet and goat cheese salad.

Nutritional Information (per serving):
Cal: 180 | Carbs: 20g | Pro: 7g | Fat: 9g
Sugars: 13g | Fiber: 5g

11. Cucumber and Tomato Salad

Preparation time: 10 minutes
Servings: 2

Ingredients:

- 1 cucumber, thinly sliced
- 2 tomatoes, diced
- 1/2 red onion, thinly sliced
- 2 tablespoons extra-virgin olive oil
- Salt and pepper to taste

Instructions:

1. In a medium bowl, combine the sliced cucumber, diced tomatoes, and thinly sliced red onion.
2. Drizzle the extra-virgin olive oil over the vegetables.
3. Season with salt and pepper to taste.
4. Toss the salad gently to coat the vegetables evenly with the dressing.
5. Serve immediately as a refreshing side dish.

Nutritional Information (per serving):
Cal: 90 | Carbs: 9g | Pro: 1g | Fat: 7g
Sugars: 4g | Fiber: 2g

12. Greek Pasta Salad

Preparation time: 10 minutes
Servings: 2

Ingredients:

- 1 cup cooked whole wheat pasta
- 1/4 cup crumbled feta cheese
- 2 tablespoons sun-dried tomatoes, chopped
- 2 tablespoons Kalamata olives, sliced
- 2 tablespoons extra-virgin olive oil

Instructions:

1. In a bowl, combine the cooked pasta, crumbled feta, chopped sun-dried tomatoes, and sliced Kalamata olives.
2. Drizzle with extra-virgin olive oil and toss until well combined.
3. Serve immediately or refrigerate for a chilled pasta salad.

Nutritional Information (per serving):
Cal: 320 | Carbs: 33g | Pro: 8g | Fat: 18g
Sugars: 2g | Fiber: 6g

13. Orange and Red Onion Salad

Preparation time: 10 minutes
Servings: 2

Ingredients:

- 2 oranges, peeled and sliced
- 1/2 red onion, thinly sliced
- 1/4 cup black olives, sliced
- 1 tablespoon extra-virgin olive oil
- Freshly ground black pepper to taste

Instructions:

1. Arrange the orange slices on a serving plate.
2. Scatter the thinly sliced red onion and sliced black olives over the oranges.
3. Drizzle extra-virgin olive oil over the salad.
4. Finish with a sprinkle of freshly ground black pepper.
5. Serve immediately for a burst of citrusy freshness.

Nutritional Information (per serving):
Cal: 140 | Carbs: 17g | Pro: 2g | Fat: 8g
Sugars: 10g | Fiber: 4g

14. Mediterranean Couscous Salad

Preparation time: 10 minutes
Servings: 2

Ingredients:

- 1 cup cooked couscous
- 1/2 cup cherry tomatoes, halved
- 1/2 cucumber, diced
- 2 tablespoons feta cheese, crumbled
- 2 tablespoons fresh lemon juice

Instructions:

1. In a bowl, combine the cooked couscous, cherry tomatoes, diced cucumber, and crumbled feta cheese.
2. Drizzle fresh lemon juice over the salad.
3. Toss gently until all ingredients are well mixed.
4. Serve immediately as a light and flavorful side dish.

Nutritional Information (per serving):
Cal: 180 | Carbs: 34g | Pro: 5g | Fat: 2g
Sugars: 2g | Fiber: 3g

15. Fattoush Salad with Sumac Dressing

Preparation time: 10 minutes
Servings: 2

Ingredients:

- 2 cups mixed salad greens
- 1 cucumber, sliced
- 1 cup cherry tomatoes, halved
- 1/4 cup fresh mint leaves, chopped
- 2 tablespoons sumac dressing

Instructions:

1. In a large bowl, combine the mixed salad greens, sliced cucumber, halved cherry tomatoes, and chopped mint leaves.
2. Drizzle sumac dressing over the salad.
3. Toss gently until the salad is evenly coated with the dressing.
4. Serve immediately for a refreshing and tangy salad.

Nutritional Information (per serving):
Cal: 80 | Carbs: 18g | Pro: 3g | Fat: 1g
Sugars: 5g | Fiber: 6g

16. Artichoke and White Bean Salad

Preparation time: 10 minutes
Servings: 2

Ingredients:

- 1 can (15 oz) white beans, drained and rinsed
- 1 cup artichoke hearts, chopped
- 2 tablespoons extra-virgin olive oil
- 1 tablespoon balsamic vinegar
- Salt and pepper to taste

Instructions:

1. In a bowl, combine the white beans and chopped artichoke hearts.
2. Drizzle with extra-virgin olive oil and balsamic vinegar.
3. Season with salt and pepper to taste.
4. Toss gently until well combined.
5. Serve as a satisfying and protein-packed salad.

Nutritional Information (per serving):
Cal: 280 | Carbs: 32g | Pro: 11g | Fat: 13g
Sugars: 1g | Fiber: 10g

17. Israeli Salad

Preparation time: 10 minutes
Servings: 2

Ingredients:

- 1 cucumber, diced
- 1 cup cherry tomatoes, quartered
- 1/2 red onion, finely chopped
- 2 tablespoons fresh parsley, chopped
- 2 tablespoons olive oil

Instructions:

1. In a bowl, combine the diced cucumber, quartered cherry tomatoes, chopped red onion, and fresh parsley.
2. Drizzle olive oil over the salad.
3. Toss gently to combine all the ingredients.
4. Serve immediately as a crisp and colorful side salad.

Nutritional Information (per serving):
Cal: 110 | Carbs: 10g | Pro: 2g | Fat: 7g

Sugars: 4g | Fiber: 2g

18. Roasted Red Pepper and Chickpea

Preparation time: 10 minutes
Servings: 2

Ingredients:

- 1 can (15 oz) chickpeas, drained and rinsed
- 1 cup roasted red peppers, sliced
- 2 tablespoons feta cheese, crumbled
- 2 tablespoons extra-virgin olive oil
- Salt and pepper to taste

Instructions:

1. In a bowl, combine the chickpeas, sliced roasted red peppers, and crumbled feta cheese.
2. Drizzle with extra-virgin olive oil.
3. Season with salt and pepper to taste.
4. Toss gently until all ingredients are well incorporated.
5. Serve as a flavorful and protein-rich salad.

Nutritional Information (per serving):
Cal: 260 | Carbs: 33g | Pro: 11g | Fat: 11g
Sugars: 7g | Fiber: 10g

19. Spinach and Strawberry Salad

Preparation time: 10 minutes
Servings: 2

Ingredients:

- 2 cups fresh spinach leaves
- 1 cup strawberries, hulled and sliced
- 1/4 cup crumbled feta cheese
- 2 tablespoons balsamic vinaigrette
- 1 tablespoon chopped walnuts (optional)

Instructions:

1. In a large bowl, combine the fresh spinach leaves, sliced strawberries, and crumbled feta cheese.
2. Drizzle with balsamic vinaigrette.
3. Toss gently until the salad is evenly coated with the dressing.
4. Optionally, sprinkle chopped walnuts on top for added crunch.

5. Serve immediately as a sweet and savory salad.

Nutritional Information (per serving):
Cal: 120 | Carbs: 14g | Pro: 4g | Fat: 7g
Sugars: 8g | Fiber: 4g

20. Grilled Vegetable Salad with Feta

Preparation time: 10 minutes
Servings: 2

Ingredients:

- 2 cups mixed grilled vegetables (zucchini, bell peppers, eggplant)
- 1/4 cup crumbled feta cheese
- 2 tablespoons pesto sauce
- 2 tablespoons extra-virgin olive oil
- Salt and pepper to taste

Instructions:

1. Prepare the mixed grilled vegetables on a grill or grill pan.
2. In a bowl, combine the grilled vegetables and crumbled feta cheese.
3. Drizzle with pesto sauce and extra-virgin olive oil.
4. Season with salt and pepper to taste.
5. Toss gently until all ingredients are well combined.
6. Serve immediately as a warm and flavorful grilled vegetable salad.

Nutritional Information (per serving):
Cal: 250 | Carbs: 14g | Pro: 4g | Fat: 20g
Sugars: 6g | Fiber: 4g

Snacks and Appetizers

1. Marinated Olives with Citrus & Herbs

Preparation time: 10 minutes
Servings: 2

Ingredients:

- 1 cup mixed olives (green and black)
- Zest of 1 lemon
- Zest of 1 orange
- 2 tablespoons fresh herbs (such as rosemary and thyme), finely chopped
- 2 tablespoons extra virgin olive oil

Instructions:

1. In a bowl, combine the mixed olives, lemon zest, orange zest, and chopped fresh herbs.
2. Drizzle extra virgin olive oil over the olives and herbs mixture.
3. Toss everything together until the olives are well coated with the citrus zest, herbs, and olive oil.
4. Let it marinate for at least 5 minutes to allow the flavors to meld.
5. Serve in a small dish and enjoy the citrus-infused marinated olives.

Nutritional Information (per serving):
Cal: 120 | Carbs: 2g | Pro: 0g | Fat: 13g
Sugars: 0g | Fiber: 2g

2. Roasted Red Pepper Hummus

Preparation time: 10 minutes
Servings: 2

Ingredients:

- 1 cup canned chickpeas, drained
- 1/2 cup roasted red peppers (from a jar)
- 2 tablespoons tahini
- 1 clove garlic
- Pita chips (for serving)

Instructions:

1. In a food processor, combine chickpeas, roasted red peppers, tahini, and garlic.
2. Blend until smooth, adding a little water if needed for the desired consistency.
3. Season with salt and pepper to taste.
4. Serve the roasted red pepper hummus with pita chips.

Nutritional Information (per serving):
Cal: 150 | Carbs: 18g | Pro: 5g | Fat: 8g
Sugars: 2g | Fiber: 4g

3. Greek Spanakopita Triangles

Preparation time: 10 minutes
Servings: 2

Ingredients:

- 4 sheets phyllo dough
- 1 cup frozen chopped spinach, thawed and drained
- 1/2 cup feta cheese, crumbled
- 2 tablespoons olive oil

Instructions:

1. Preheat the oven to 375°F (190°C).
2. Lay out one sheet of phyllo dough and brush it lightly with olive oil. Place another sheet on top.
3. Mix the spinach and feta, then spoon half the mixture onto one end of the phyllo sheets.
4. Fold the phyllo over the filling to create a triangle. Continue folding until the entire strip is used.
5. Repeat the process with the remaining phyllo sheets and filling.
6. Place the triangles on a baking sheet and bake for 8-10 minutes or until golden brown.
7. Serve warm.

Nutritional Information (per serving):
Cal: 280 | Carbs: 23g | Pro: 8g | Fat: 18g
Sugars: 2g | Fiber: 3g

4. Stuffed Grape Leaves with Tzatziki

Preparation time: 10 minutes
Servings: 2

Ingredients:

- 10 grape leaves (canned or jarred), drained
- 1/2 cup cooked rice
- 2 tablespoons pine nuts
- 2 tablespoons tzatziki sauce

Instructions:

1. In a bowl, mix the cooked rice and pine nuts.
2. Lay out a grape leaf, place a small portion

of the rice mixture in the center, and roll it tightly.
3. Repeat with the remaining grape leaves.
4. Serve the stuffed grape leaves with a side of tzatziki sauce for dipping.

Nutritional Information (per serving):
Cal: 180 | Carbs: 25g | Pro: 3g | Fat: 8g
Sugars: 1g | Fiber: 2g

5. Baked Feta with Honey & Walnuts

Preparation time: 10 minutes
Servings: 2

Ingredients:

* 1/2 cup feta cheese, block or sliced
* 2 tablespoons honey
* 2 tablespoons chopped walnuts

Instructions:

1. Preheat the oven to 350°F (175°C).
2. Place the feta in an oven-safe dish.
3. Drizzle honey over the feta and sprinkle chopped walnuts on top.
4. Bake for 5-7 minutes or until the feta is warm and slightly melted.
5. Serve immediately, spreading the honey and walnuts over each bite.

Nutritional Information (per serving):
Cal: 220 | Carbs: 15g | Pro: 8g | Fat: 15g
Sugars: 14g | Fiber: 1g

6. Mediterranean Bruschetta

Preparation time: 10 minutes
Servings: 2

Ingredients:

* 4 slices whole grain baguette
* 1 cup cherry tomatoes, diced
* 2 tablespoons fresh basil, chopped
* 2 tablespoons balsamic glaze

Instructions:

1. Toast the slices of whole grain baguette until golden brown.
2. In a bowl, mix diced cherry tomatoes and chopped fresh basil.

3. Spoon the tomato and basil mixture onto each slice of toasted baguette.
4. Drizzle balsamic glaze over the bruschetta before serving.

Nutritional Information (per serving):
Cal: 180 | Carbs: 35g | Pro: 5g | Fat: 1g
Sugars: 8g | Fiber: 4g

7. Cucumber and Feta Bites

Preparation time: 10 minutes
Servings: 2

Ingredients:

* 1 cucumber, sliced
* 1/2 cup feta cheese, crumbled
* 2 tablespoons fresh dill, chopped
* Black pepper (to taste)

Instructions:

1. Arrange cucumber slices on a serving platter.
2. Sprinkle crumbled feta over each cucumber slice.
3. Garnish with fresh chopped dill.
4. Finish with a dash of black pepper.
5. Serve these refreshing bites immediately.

Nutritional Information (per serving):
Cal: 110 | Carbs: 6g | Pro: 5g | Fat: 8g
Sugars: 4g | Fiber: 2g

8. Artichoke and Spinach Dip

Preparation time: 10 minutes
Servings: 2

Ingredients:

* 1 cup frozen chopped spinach, thawed and drained
* 1/2 cup canned artichoke hearts, chopped
* 1/2 cup mayonnaise
* 1/4 cup grated Parmesan cheese

Instructions:

1. In a bowl, combine chopped spinach, chopped artichoke hearts, mayonnaise, and grated Parmesan cheese.
2. Mix until well combined.
3. Microwave the mixture for 2-3 minutes or until

4. Stir and serve with your favorite dippables.

Nutritional Information (per serving):
Cal: 350 | Carbs: 6g | Pro: 4g | Fat: 34g
Sugars: 1g | Fiber: 3g

9. Grilled Halloumi Cheese Skewers

Preparation time: 10 minutes
Servings: 2

Ingredients:

- 8 cubes of halloumi cheese
- 1 tablespoon olive oil
- 1 teaspoon dried oregano
- Lemon wedges (for serving)

Instructions:

1. Preheat the grill or grill pan over medium heat.
2. Thread halloumi cubes onto skewers.
3. Brush the halloumi skewers with olive oil and sprinkle with dried oregano.
4. Grill for 2-3 minutes on each side or until grill marks appear.
5. Serve with lemon wedges for a burst of citrus flavor.

Nutritional Information (per serving):
Cal: 220 | Carbs: 2g | Pro: 14g | Fat: 18g
Sugars: 1g | Fiber: 0g

10. Eggplant and Tomato Crostini

Preparation time: 10 minutes
Servings: 2

Ingredients:

- 4 slices whole grain baguette
- 1/2 medium eggplant, diced
- 1 cup cherry tomatoes, halved
- 2 tablespoons balsamic glaze

Instructions:

1. Toast the slices of whole grain baguette until golden brown.
2. In a skillet, sauté diced eggplant until tender.
3. Top each slice of baguette with sautéed eggplant and halved cherry tomatoes.

4. Drizzle balsamic glaze over the crostini before serving.

Nutritional Information (per serving):
Cal: 180 | Carbs: 35g | Pro: 5g | Fat: 1g
Sugars: 8g | Fiber: 4g

11. Greek Yogurt and Herb Dip

Preparation time: 5 minutes
Servings: 2

Ingredients:

- 1 cup Greek yogurt
- 2 tablespoons fresh dill, chopped
- 1 tablespoon fresh mint, chopped
- 1 clove garlic, minced
- Salt and pepper to taste

Instructions:

1. In a bowl, combine Greek yogurt, chopped dill, chopped mint, and minced garlic.
2. Mix the ingredients thoroughly until well combined.
3. Season with salt and pepper to taste. Adjust the seasoning if necessary.
4. Serve immediately with pita chips, vegetable sticks, or as a dip for your favorite snacks.

Nutritional Information (per serving):
Cal: 70 | Carbs: 4g | Pro: 10g | Fat: 1g
Sugars: 3g | Fiber: 0g

12. Mediterranean Quesadillas

Preparation time: 10 minutes
Servings: 2

Ingredients:

- 4 whole wheat tortillas
- 1 cup hummus
- 1 cup cherry tomatoes, halved
- 1/2 cup feta cheese, crumbled

Instructions:

1. Spread hummus evenly over two of the tortillas.
2. Top with cherry tomatoes and crumbled feta.
3. Place the remaining tortillas on top to create a quesadilla.

4. Heat a non-stick pan over medium heat and cook each quesadilla for 2-3 minutes on each side or until the tortilla is golden brown and the filling is warmed through.
5. Slice into wedges and serve immediately.

Nutritional Information (per serving):
Cal: 380 | Carbs: 42g | Pro: 14g | Fat: 18g
Sugars: 3g | Fiber: 7g

13. Olive and Herb Focaccia Bread

Preparation time: 10 minutes
Servings: 2

Ingredients:

- 2 pieces of store-bought focaccia bread
- 2 tablespoons extra virgin olive oil
- 1 tablespoon fresh rosemary, chopped
- 1/4 cup mixed olives, sliced

Instructions:

1. Preheat the oven according to the focaccia package instructions.
2. Place the focaccia on a baking sheet.
3. Drizzle each piece with olive oil, ensuring even coverage.
4. Sprinkle chopped rosemary and sliced olives over the top.
5. Bake in the preheated oven according to the package instructions until the bread is golden and crispy.
6. Slice and serve warm.

Nutritional Information (per serving):
Cal: 350 | Carbs: 40g | Pro: 8g | Fat: 18g
Sugars: 0g | Fiber: 2g

14. Spicy Harissa Roasted Chickpeas

Preparation time: 5 minutes
Servings: 2

Ingredients:

- 1 can (15 oz) chickpeas, drained and rinsed
- 2 tablespoons olive oil
- 1 tablespoon harissa paste
- Salt to taste

Instructions:

1. Preheat the oven to 400°F (200°C).
2. In a bowl, toss chickpeas with olive oil, harissa paste, and salt until evenly coated.
3. Spread the chickpeas on a baking sheet in a single layer.
4. Roast in the preheated oven for 20-25 minutes or until crispy, shaking the pan halfway through.
5. Allow the roasted chickpeas to cool slightly before serving.

Nutritional Information (per serving):
Cal: 320 | Carbs: 35g | Pro: 11g | Fat: 16g
Sugars: 6g | Fiber: 10g

15. Baked Zucchini Fries with Tzatziki

Preparation time: 10 minutes
Servings: 2

Ingredients:

- 2 medium zucchinis, cut into fries
- 1/4 cup breadcrumbs
- 1 teaspoon dried oregano
- Salt and pepper to taste
- 1/2 cup tzatziki sauce for dipping

Instructions:

1. Preheat the oven to 425°F (220°C).
2. In a bowl, combine zucchini fries with breadcrumbs, dried oregano, salt, and pepper. Toss until evenly coated.
3. Place the coated zucchini on a baking sheet lined with parchment paper.
4. Bake for 20-25 minutes or until golden and crispy, turning halfway through.
5. Serve hot with tzatziki sauce for dipping.

Nutritional Information (per serving):
Cal: 120 | Carbs: 23g | Pro: 5g | Fat: 2g
Sugars: 5g | Fiber: 4g

16. Tomato Basil Bruschetta

Preparation time: 10 minutes
Servings: 2

Ingredients:

- 4 slices of whole grain baguette
- 2 large tomatoes, diced
- 1/4 cup fresh basil, chopped

- 2 tablespoons extra virgin olive oil
- Salt and pepper to taste

Instructions:

1. Toast the slices of whole grain baguette until golden brown.
2. In a bowl, combine diced tomatoes, chopped basil, olive oil, salt, and pepper.
3. Spoon the tomato mixture over the toasted baguette slices.
4. Serve immediately as a light and flavorful appetizer.

Nutritional Information (per serving):
Cal: 160 | Carbs: 20g | Pro: 4g | Fat: 8g
Sugars: 3g | Fiber: 3g

17. Feta & Olive Stuffed Mini Peppers

Preparation time: 10 minutes
Servings: 2

Ingredients:

- 10 mini sweet peppers, halved and seeds removed
- 1/2 cup feta cheese, crumbled
- 1/4 cup Kalamata olives, chopped
- 1 tablespoon fresh parsley, chopped

Instructions:

1. Preheat the oven to 375°F (190°C).
2. In a bowl, mix together crumbled feta, chopped Kalamata olives, and fresh parsley.
3. Stuff each mini pepper half with the feta and olive mixture.
4. Place the stuffed peppers on a baking sheet and bake for 8-10 minutes or until the peppers are tender.
5. Serve warm as a delightful appetizer.

Nutritional Information (per serving):
Cal: 150 | Carbs: 10g | Pro: 6g | Fat: 11g
Sugars: 5g | Fiber: 2g

18. Roasted Garlic & White Bean Dip

Preparation time: 10 minutes
Servings: 2

Ingredients:

- 1 can (15 oz) white beans, drained and rinsed
- 2 cloves garlic, roasted
- 2 tablespoons extra virgin olive oil
- Salt and pepper to taste

Instructions:

1. In a blender or food processor, combine white beans, roasted garlic, and olive oil.
2. Blend until smooth, adding a little water if needed to achieve the desired consistency.
3. Season with salt and pepper to taste.
4. Serve with fresh vegetable sticks or whole grain crackers.

Nutritional Information (per serving):
Cal: 220 | Carbs: 27g | Pro: 8g | Fat: 9g
Sugars: 0g | Fiber: 6g

19. Greek-Style Stuffed Mushrooms

Preparation time: 10 minutes
Servings: 2

Ingredients:

- 8 large white mushrooms, stems removed and chopped
- 1/2 cup feta cheese, crumbled
- 2 tablespoons fresh parsley, chopped
- 2 tablespoons breadcrumbs

Instructions:

1. Preheat the oven to 375°F (190°C).
2. In a bowl, mix together chopped mushroom stems, feta cheese, fresh parsley, and breadcrumbs.
3. Stuff each mushroom cap with the mixture.
4. Place the stuffed mushrooms on a baking sheet and bake for 12-15 minutes or until the mushrooms are tender.
5. Serve as a savory and satisfying appetizer.

Nutritional Information (per serving):
Cal: 160 | Carbs: 9g | Pro: 9g | Fat: 11g
Sugars: 2g | Fiber: 2g

20. Smoked Salmon & Cucumber Bites

Preparation time: 10 minutes
Servings: 2

Ingredients:

- 8 cucumber slices
- 4 oz smoked salmon
- 2 tablespoons cream cheese
- Fresh dill for garnish

Instructions:

1. Lay out the cucumber slices on a serving platter.
2. Spread a thin layer of cream cheese on each cucumber slice.
3. Top each slice with a piece of smoked salmon.
4. Garnish with fresh dill.
5. Serve immediately as elegant and refreshing appetizers.

Nutritional Information (per serving):
Cal: 180 | Carbs: 4g | Pro: 12g | Fat: 12g
Sugars: 2g | Fiber: 1g

Desserts

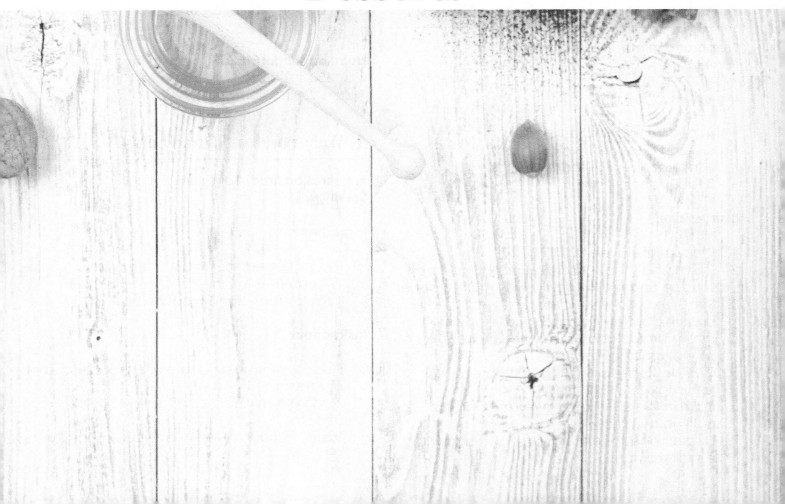

1. Greek Yogurt with Honey & Pistachios

Preparation time: 5 minutes
Servings: 2

Ingredients:

- 2 cups Greek yogurt
- 4 tablespoons honey
- 1/4 cup chopped pistachios

Instructions:

1. Divide the Greek yogurt equally between two serving bowls.
2. Drizzle 2 tablespoons of honey over each bowl of yogurt.
3. Sprinkle the chopped pistachios evenly over the yogurt and honey.
4. Gently stir the ingredients together to combine.
5. Serve immediately and enjoy the creamy goodness!

Nutritional Information (per serving):
Cal: 320 | Carbs: 36g | Pro: 19g | Fat: 13g
Sugars: 31g | Fiber: 2g

2. Baklava with Walnuts and Honey

Preparation time: 10 minutes
Servings: 2

Ingredients:

- 4 sheets of phyllo pastry
- 1/2 cup chopped walnuts
- 4 tablespoons melted butter
- 3 tablespoons honey

Instructions:

1. Preheat the oven to 350°F (175°C).
2. Place one sheet of phyllo pastry on a clean surface and brush it lightly with melted butter.
3. Sprinkle a portion of chopped walnuts evenly over the buttered phyllo sheet.
4. Repeat the process with three more layers of phyllo, creating a stack.
5. Cut the stacked phyllo into squares or rectangles.
6. Bake in the preheated oven for 10 minutes or until golden brown.
7. Drizzle honey over the baked baklava while it's still warm.

8. Allow it to cool slightly before serving.

Nutritional Information (per serving):
Cal: 420 | Carbs: 33g | Pro: 7g | Fat: 30g
Sugars: 16g | Fiber: 3g

3. Orange and Almond Flourless Cake

Preparation time: 10 minutes
Servings: 2

Ingredients:

- 1 cup almond meal
- 2 large eggs
- 1/4 cup honey
- Zest of 1 orange

Instructions:

1. Preheat the oven to 350°F (175°C) and grease two small baking pans.
2. In a bowl, whisk together almond meal, eggs, honey, and orange zest until well combined.
3. Pour the batter into the prepared pans, dividing it evenly.
4. Bake for 20-25 minutes or until a toothpick inserted comes out clean.
5. Allow the cakes to cool before slicing and serving.

Nutritional Information (per serving):
Cal: 380 | Carbs: 30g | Pro: 12g | Fat: 24g
Sugars: 24g | Fiber: 4g

4. Watermelon Mint Sorbet

Preparation time: 10 minutes
Servings: 2

Ingredients:

- 4 cups cubed seedless watermelon
- 1/4 cup fresh mint leaves
- 1 tablespoon honey (optional)

Instructions:

1. Place watermelon cubes in a blender or food processor.
2. Add fresh mint leaves and blend until smooth.
3. Taste and add honey if a sweeter sorbet is desired.

3. Pour the mixture into a shallow dish and freeze for at least 4 hours, stirring every hour.
4. Scoop into bowls, garnish with mint leaves, and enjoy the refreshing sorbet.

Nutritional Information (per serving):
Cal: 100 | Carbs: 26g | Pro: 2g | Fat: 0g
Sugars: 22g | Fiber: 2g

5. Chocolate and Olive Oil Mousse

Preparation time: 10 minutes
Servings: 2

Ingredients:

- 1/2 cup dark chocolate chips
- 2 tablespoons extra virgin olive oil
- 1/4 cup warm water
- Pinch of sea salt

Instructions:

1. Melt the dark chocolate chips in a heatproof bowl over simmering water or in the microwave.
2. Stir in the olive oil and warm water until smooth.
3. Add a pinch of sea salt and mix well.
4. Pour the mousse into serving glasses and refrigerate for at least 2 hours.
5. Garnish with a sprinkle of sea salt before serving.

Nutritional Information (per serving):
Cal: 320 | Carbs: 28g | Pro: 3g | Fat: 23g
Sugars: 20g | Fiber: 3g

6. Lemon Ricotta Pancakes with Berries

Preparation time: 10 minutes
Servings: 2

Ingredients:

- 1 cup ricotta cheese
- 2 large eggs
- Zest of 1 lemon
- Fresh berries for topping

Instructions:

1. In a bowl, whisk together ricotta, eggs, and lemon zest until smooth.

2. Heat a non-stick skillet over medium heat.
3. Spoon the pancake batter onto the skillet, forming small pancakes.
4. Cook until bubbles form on the surface, then flip and cook the other side.
5. Serve with fresh berries on top.

Nutritional Information (per serving):
Cal: 320 | Carbs: 10g | Pro: 19g | Fat: 24g
Sugars: 3g | Fiber: 0g

7. Fig and Walnut Biscotti

Preparation time: 10 minutes
Servings: 2

Ingredients:

- 1 cup all-purpose flour
- 1/2 cup dried figs, chopped
- 1/2 cup walnuts, chopped
- 1/4 cup sugar
- 1/2 teaspoon baking powder

Instructions:

1. Preheat the oven to 350°F (175°C).
2. In a bowl, mix together flour, chopped figs, walnuts, sugar, and baking powder.
3. Form the dough into a log and place it on a baking sheet.
4. Bake for 20-25 minutes until golden brown.
5. Allow the log to cool slightly before slicing into biscotti.
6. Place the biscotti back in the oven for 5 minutes on each side.
7. Cool completely before serving.

Nutritional Information (per serving):
Cal: 450 | Carbs: 63g | Pro: 8g | Fat: 20g
Sugars: 22g | Fiber: 4g

8. Greek Honey Cake (Melopita)

Preparation time: 10 minutes
Servings: 2

Ingredients:

- 1 cup Greek yogurt
- 2 tablespoons honey
- 1 cup crushed honey graham crackers
- 1 teaspoon cinnamon

Instructions:

1. In a bowl, mix Greek yogurt, honey, crushed graham crackers, and cinnamon until well combined.
2. Divide the mixture into two serving glasses.
3. Refrigerate for at least 1 hour before serving.

Nutritional Information (per serving):
Cal: 280 | Carbs: 40g | Pro: 9g | Fat: 9g
Sugars: 23g | Fiber: 2g

9. Pistachio & Rosewater Semolina Cake

Preparation time: 10 minutes
Servings: 2

Ingredients:

- 1 cup semolina
- 1/2 cup crushed pistachios
- 2 tablespoons honey
- 1 teaspoon rosewater

Instructions:

1. In a bowl, mix semolina, crushed pistachios, honey, and rosewater until well combined.
2. Press the mixture into small cake molds or serving glasses.
3. Refrigerate for at least 2 hours before serving.

Nutritional Information (per serving):
Cal: 320 | Carbs: 60g | Pro: 7g | Fat: 7g
Sugars: 24g | Fiber: 3g

10. Roasted Apricots with Greek Yogurt

Preparation time: 10 minutes
Servings: 2

Ingredients:

- 4 fresh apricots, halved and pitted
- 2 tablespoons honey
- 1/4 cup chopped pistachios
- 1 cup Greek yogurt

Instructions:

1. Preheat the oven to 400°F (200°C).
2. Place apricot halves on a baking sheet.
3. Drizzle honey over the apricots and roast for 5-7 minutes.

4. Serve the roasted apricots over Greek yogurt.
5. Sprinkle chopped pistachios on top and enjoy!

Nutritional Information (per serving):
Cal: 260 | Carbs: 34g | Pro: 13g | Fat: 9g
Sugars: 23g | Fiber: 4g

11. Almond & Orange Blossom Cookies

Preparation time: 10 minutes
Servings: 2

Ingredients:

- 1 cup almond flour
- 1/4 cup honey
- 1 teaspoon orange blossom water
- 1/4 teaspoon almond extract
- Pinch of salt

Instructions:

1. Preheat the oven to 350°F (175°C) and line a baking sheet with parchment paper.
2. In a bowl, mix almond flour, honey, orange blossom water, almond extract, and a pinch of salt until well combined.
3. Scoop out small portions of the dough and shape them into cookies.
4. Place the cookies on the prepared baking sheet and flatten them slightly with a fork.
5. Bake for 8-10 minutes or until the edges are golden brown.
6. Allow the cookies to cool on the baking sheet for a few minutes before transferring them to a wire rack to cool completely.

Nutritional Information (per serving):
Cal: 260 | Carbs: 24g | Pro: 7g | Fat: 17g
Sugars: 17g | Fiber: 4g

12. Chocolate Dipped Dates

Preparation time: 10 minutes
Servings: 2

Ingredients:

- 10 Medjool dates, pitted
- 2 ounces dark chocolate, melted
- Sea salt, for sprinkling

Instructions:

1. Line a plate or tray with parchment paper.
2. Dip each pitted date into the melted dark chocolate, coating them halfway.
3. Place the chocolate-dipped dates on the parchment paper.
4. Sprinkle a pinch of sea salt over each chocolate-covered date.
5. Allow the chocolate to set at room temperature or speed up the process by placing them in the refrigerator for a few minutes.

Nutritional Information (per serving):
Cal: 210 | Carbs: 48g | Pro: 2g | Fat: 4g
Sugars: 42g | Fiber: 5g

13. Greek Rice Pudding (Rizogalo)

Preparation time: 10 minutes
Servings: 2

Ingredients:

- 1/2 cup Arborio rice
- 2 cups milk
- 1/4 cup honey
- 1/2 teaspoon vanilla extract
- Ground cinnamon, for garnish

Instructions:

1. In a saucepan, combine rice, milk, honey, and vanilla extract.
2. Bring the mixture to a gentle boil, then reduce the heat to low.
3. Simmer, stirring occasionally, for about 8-10 minutes or until the rice is tender and the mixture has thickened.
4. Remove from heat and let it cool for a few minutes.
5. Divide the rice pudding into serving bowls, sprinkle with ground cinnamon, and serve warm.

Nutritional Information (per serving):
Cal: 370 | Carbs: 73g | Pro: 9g | Fat: 6g
Sugars: 32g | Fiber: 1g

14. Mediterranean Fruit Salad

Preparation time: 10 minutes
Servings: 2

Ingredients:

- 1 cup mixed fresh berries (strawberries, blueberries, raspberries)
- 1 orange, peeled and segmented
- 1 tablespoon honey
- Fresh mint leaves, for garnish

Instructions:

1. In a bowl, gently toss together the mixed berries and orange segments.
2. Drizzle honey over the fruit and toss again until well coated.
3. Divide the fruit salad into two serving bowls.
4. Garnish with fresh mint leaves.
5. Serve immediately.

Nutritional Information (per serving):
Cal: 120 | Carbs: 30g | Pro: 2g | Fat: 0g
Sugars: 25g | Fiber: 5g

15. Lemon Olive Oil Cake

Preparation time: 10 minutes
Servings: 2

Ingredients:

- 1 cup almond flour
- 2 tablespoons lemon juice
- 2 tablespoons olive oil
- 2 tablespoons honey
- 1/2 teaspoon baking powder

Instructions:

1. Preheat the oven to 350°F (175°C) and grease a small baking dish.
2. In a bowl, combine almond flour, lemon juice, olive oil, honey, and baking powder.
3. Mix until the batter is smooth.
4. Pour the batter into the greased baking dish.
5. Bake for 15-18 minutes or until a toothpick inserted into the center comes out clean.
6. Allow the cake to cool before slicing and serving.

Nutritional Information (per serving):
Cal: 480 | Carbs: 28g | Pro: 10g | Fat: 38g
Sugars: 19g | Fiber: 6g

16. Walnut and Honey Phyllo Pastry

Preparation time: 10 minutes
Servings: 2

Ingredients:

- 4 sheets phyllo pastry
- 1/2 cup chopped walnuts
- 2 tablespoons honey
- 2 tablespoons melted butter

Instructions:

1. Preheat the oven to 350°F (175°C).
2. Place one sheet of phyllo pastry on a clean surface and brush it lightly with melted butter.
3. Sprinkle a portion of chopped walnuts over the pastry.
4. Repeat the process, layering three more sheets of phyllo with butter and walnuts.
5. Drizzle honey over the top layer.
6. Bake for 10-12 minutes or until golden brown.
7. Allow it to cool for a few minutes before slicing.

Nutritional Information (per serving):
Cal: 420 | Carbs: 38g | Pro: 7g | Fat: 28g
Sugars: 16g | Fiber: 4g

17. Ricotta and Honey Stuffed Figs

Preparation time: 10 minutes
Servings: 2

Ingredients:

- 4 fresh figs, halved
- 1/2 cup ricotta cheese
- 2 tablespoons honey
- Chopped pistachios, for garnish

Instructions:

1. In a bowl, mix ricotta cheese and honey until well combined.
2. Spoon a small amount of the ricotta mixture into each fig half.
3. Drizzle honey over the stuffed figs.
4. Garnish with chopped pistachios.
5. Serve immediately.

Nutritional Information (per serving):
Cal: 270 | Carbs: 40g | Pro: 7g | Fat: 11g
Sugars: 30g | Fiber: 6g

18. Pistachio and Honey Baklava Cups

Preparation time: 10 minutes

Servings: 2

Ingredients:

- 6 phyllo pastry sheets, cut into squares
- 1/2 cup chopped pistachios
- 2 tablespoons honey
- 2 tablespoons melted butter

Instructions:

1. Preheat the oven to 350°F (175°C).
2. Place phyllo pastry squares into a muffin tin, brushing each layer with melted butter.
3. Layer chopped pistachios over the phyllo in each cup.
4. Repeat the process, layering phyllo, butter, and pistachios until the cups are filled.
5. Bake for 10-12 minutes or until golden brown.
6. Drizzle honey over each baklava cup while still warm.

Nutritional Information (per serving):
Cal: 340 | Carbs: 28g | Pro: 6g | Fat: 24g
Sugars: 13g | Fiber: 4g

19. Orange & Cardamom Poached Pears

Preparation time: 10 minutes
Servings: 2

Ingredients:

- 2 ripe pears, peeled and halved
- 1 cup orange juice
- 2 tablespoons honey
- 1/2 teaspoon ground cardamom

Instructions:

1. In a saucepan, combine orange juice, honey, and ground cardamom.
2. Bring the mixture to a gentle simmer.
3. Add the pear halves to the simmering liquid.
4. Poach for 5-7 minutes or until the pears are tender.
5. Remove the pears and serve with a drizzle of the poaching liquid.

Nutritional Information (per serving):
Cal: 210 | Carbs: 54g | Pro: 2g | Fat: 0g
Sugars: 37g | Fiber: 8g

20. Yogurt & Berry Parfait with Granola

Preparation time: 10 minutes
Servings: 2

Ingredients:

- 1 cup Greek yogurt
- 1 cup mixed berries (strawberries, blueberries, raspberries)
- 1/4 cup granola
- 2 tablespoons honey

Instructions:

1. In serving glasses or bowls, layer Greek yogurt, mixed berries, and granola.
2. Repeat the layers until the glasses are filled.
3. Drizzle honey over the top layer.
4. Serve immediately and enjoy!

Nutritional Information (per serving):
Cal: 290 | Carbs: 45g | Pro: 17g | Fat: 7g
Sugars: 27g | Fiber: 5g

Meal Plan

DAY	BREAKFAST	LUNCH	DINNER
1	Greek Yogurt Parfait with Fresh Berries and Honey	Tzatziki with Pita Bread	Mediterranean Baked Cod with Lemon and Herbs
2	Mediterranean Veggie Omelette	Baba Ganoush with Crudites	Grilled Chicken Souvlaki with Tzatziki
3	Whole Grain Toast with Hummus and Tomato Slices	Greek Fava Bean Dip (Fava)	Shrimp and Feta Orzo
4	Shakshuka (Poached Eggs in Tomato Sauce)	Mediterranean Hummus Platter	Eggplant Parmesan with Tomato Sauce
5	Feta and Spinach Breakfast Wrap	Roasted Red Pepper and Walnut Dip (Muhammara)	Lemon Herb Roasted Chicken Thighs
6	Olive and Tomato Focaccia	Stuffed Grape Leaves (Dolma)	Mediterranean Stuffed Peppers with Quinoa and Chickpeas
7	Quinoa Breakfast Bowl with Roasted Vegetables	Artichoke and White Bean Dip	Baked Falafel with Tahini Sauce
8	Orange and Almond Breakfast Couscous	Caprese Salad Skewers	Lemon Garlic Butter Grilled Salmon
9	Fig and Walnut Overnight Oats	Eggplant and Tomato Caponata	Chicken and Olive Tagine
10	Mediterranean Scrambled Tofu with Sun-Dried Tomatoes	Mediterranean Bruschetta with Tomatoes and Basil	Spanakorizo (Greek Spinach and Rice)
11	Greek-style Pancakes with Yogurt and Honey	Greek Taramasalata (Fish Roe Dip)	Tomato and Basil Baked Fish
12	Caprese Breakfast Sandwich	Roasted Red Pepper and Feta Dip	Lamb Kofta with Mint Yogurt Sauce
13	Avocado and Chickpea Toast	Olive Tapenade Crostini	Mediterranean Quinoa Bowl with Roasted Vegetables
14	Mediterranean Frittata with Olives and Feta	Melitzanosalata (Greek Eggplant Salad)	Chicken Piccata with Capers and Lemon
15	Chia Seed Pudding with Fresh Fruit	Marinated Olives with Herbs	Greek Moussaka
16	Spanakopita (Greek Spinach Pie) Muffins	Mediterranean Chickpea Salad	Lentil and Vegetable Stew
17	Almond and Date Smoothie Bowl	Spicy Feta and Roasted Red Pepper Dip	Swordfish Skewers with Citrus Marinade
18	Whole Grain Breakfast Burrito with Salsa	Labneh with Za'atar and Olive Oil	Mediterranean Zucchini Noodles with Pesto
19	Olive and Tomato Breakfast Bruschetta	Mediterranean Antipasto Platter	Beef and Eggplant Casserole
20	Smoked Salmon and Dill Bagel with Cream Cheese	Greek-style Tzatziki Deviled Eggs	Stuffed Acorn Squash with Mediterranean Quinoa
21	Greek Yogurt Parfait with Fresh Berries and Honey	Tzatziki with Pita Bread	Grilled Chicken Souvlaki with Tzatziki
22	Mediterranean Veggie Omelette	Baba Ganoush with Crudites	Shrimp and Feta Orzo
23	Whole Grain Toast with Hummus and Tomato Slices	Greek Fava Bean Dip (Fava)	Eggplant Parmesan with Tomato Sauce
24	Shakshuka (Poached Eggs in Tomato Sauce)	Mediterranean Hummus Platter	Lemon Herb Roasted Chicken Thighs
25	Feta and Spinach Breakfast Wrap	Roasted Red Pepper and Walnut Dip (Muhammara)	Mediterranean Stuffed Peppers with Quinoa and Chickpeas
26	Olive and Tomato Focaccia	Stuffed Grape Leaves (Dolma)	Baked Falafel with Tahini Sauce
27	Quinoa Breakfast Bowl with Roasted Vegetables	Artichoke and White Bean Dip	Lemon Garlic Butter Grilled Salmon
28	Orange and Almond Breakfast Couscous	Caprese Salad Skewers	Chicken and Olive Tagine

DAY	BREAKFAST	LUNCH	DINNER
29	Fig and Walnut Overnight Oats	Eggplant and Tomato Caponata	Spanakorizo (Greek Spinach and Rice)
30	Mediterranean Scrambled Tofu with Sun-Dried Tomatoes	Mediterranean Bruschetta with Tomatoes and Basil	Tomato and Basil Baked Fish
31	Greek-style Pancakes with Yogurt and Honey	Greek Taramasalata (Fish Roe Dip)	Lamb Kofta with Mint Yogurt Sauce
32	Caprese Breakfast Sandwich	Roasted Red Pepper and Feta Dip	Mediterranean Quinoa Bowl with Roasted Vegetables
33	Avocado and Chickpea Toast	Olive Tapenade Crostini	Chicken Piccata with Capers and Lemon
34	Mediterranean Frittata with Olives and Feta	Melitzanosalata (Greek Eggplant Salad)	Greek Moussaka
35	Chia Seed Pudding with Fresh Fruit	Marinated Olives with Herbs	Lentil and Vegetable Stew
36	Spanakopita (Greek Spinach Pie) Muffins	Mediterranean Chickpea Salad	Swordfish Skewers with Citrus Marinade
37	Almond and Date Smoothie Bowl	Spicy Feta and Roasted Red Pepper Dip	Mediterranean Zucchini Noodles with Pesto
38	Whole Grain Breakfast Burrito with Salsa	Labneh with Za'atar and Olive Oil	Beef and Eggplant Casserole
39	Olive and Tomato Breakfast Bruschetta	Mediterranean Antipasto Platter	Stuffed Acorn Squash with Mediterranean Quinoa
40	Smoked Salmon and Dill Bagel with Cream Cheese	Greek-style Tzatziki Deviled Eggs	Greek Baked Meatballs (Keftedes) with Tomato Sauce
41	Greek Yogurt Parfait with Fresh Berries and Honey	Tzatziki with Pita Bread	Grilled Chicken Souvlaki with Tzatziki
42	Mediterranean Veggie Omelette	Baba Ganoush with Crudites	Shrimp and Feta Orzo
43	Whole Grain Toast with Hummus and Tomato Slices	Greek Fava Bean Dip (Fava)	Eggplant Parmesan with Tomato Sauce
44	Shakshuka (Poached Eggs in Tomato Sauce)	Mediterranean Hummus Platter	Lemon Herb Roasted Chicken Thighs
45	Feta and Spinach Breakfast Wrap	Roasted Red Pepper and Walnut Dip (Muhammara)	Mediterranean Stuffed Peppers with Quinoa and Chickpeas
46	Olive and Tomato Focaccia	Stuffed Grape Leaves (Dolma)	Baked Falafel with Tahini Sauce
47	Quinoa Breakfast Bowl with Roasted Vegetables	Artichoke and White Bean Dip	Lemon Garlic Butter Grilled Salmon
48	Orange and Almond Breakfast Couscous	Caprese Salad Skewers	Chicken and Olive Tagine
49	Fig and Walnut Overnight Oats	Eggplant and Tomato Caponata	Spanakorizo (Greek Spinach and Rice)
50	Mediterranean Scrambled Tofu with Sun-Dried Tomatoes	Mediterranean Bruschetta with Tomatoes and Basil	Tomato and Basil Baked Fish
51	Greek-style Pancakes with Yogurt and Honey	Greek Taramasalata (Fish Roe Dip)	Lamb Kofta with Mint Yogurt Sauce
52	Caprese Breakfast Sandwich	Roasted Red Pepper and Feta Dip	Mediterranean Quinoa Bowl with Roasted Vegetables
53	Avocado and Chickpea Toast	Olive Tapenade Crostini	Chicken Piccata with Capers and Lemon
54	Mediterranean Frittata with Olives and Feta	Melitzanosalata (Greek Eggplant Salad)	Greek Moussaka
55	Chia Seed Pudding with Fresh Fruit	Marinated Olives with Herbs	Lentil and Vegetable Stew
56	Spanakopita (Greek Spinach Pie) Muffins	Mediterranean Chickpea Salad	Swordfish Skewers with Citrus Marinade

DAY	BREAKFAST	LUNCH	DINNER
57	Almond and Date Smoothie Bowl	Spicy Feta and Roasted Red Pepper Dip	Mediterranean Zucchini Noodles with Pesto
58	Whole Grain Breakfast Burrito with Salsa	Labneh with Za'atar and Olive Oil	Beef and Eggplant Casserole
59	Olive and Tomato Breakfast Bruschetta	Mediterranean Antipasto Platter	Stuffed Acorn Squash with Mediterranean Quinoa
60	Smoked Salmon and Dill Bagel with Cream Cheese	Greek-style Tzatziki Deviled Eggs	Greek Baked Meatballs (Keftedes) with Tomato Sauce

Conversion Tables

WEIGHT EQUIVALENTS

US STANDARD	METRIC (APPROXIMATE)
1 Ounce	28 g
2 Ounces	57 g
5 Ounces	142 g
10 Ounces	284 g
15 Ounces	425 g
16 Ounces (1 Pound)	455g
1.5 Pounds	680 g
2 Pounds	907 g

VOLUME EQUIVALENTS (DRY)

US STANDARD	METRIC (APPROXIMATE)
1/8 Teaspoon	0.5 ml
1/4 Teaspoon	1 ml
1/2 Teaspoon	2 ml
3/4 Teaspoon	4 ml
1 Teaspoon	5 ml
1 Tablespoon	15 ml
1/4 Cup	59 ml
1/2 Cup	118 ml
3/4 Cup	177 ml
1 Cup	235 ml
2 Cups	475 ml
3 Cups	700 ml
4 Cups	1 l

VOLUME EQUIVALENTS (LIQUID)

US STANDARD	US STANDARD (OUNCES)	METRIC (APPROXIMATE)
2 Tablespoons	1 fl.oz.	30 ml
1/4 Cup	2 fl.oz.	60 ml
1/2 Cup	4 fl.oz.	120 ml
1 Cup	8 fl.oz.	240 ml
1 1/2 Cups	12 fl.oz.	355 ml
2 Cups or 1 Pint	16 fl.oz.	475 ml
4 Cups or 1 Quart	32 fl.oz.	1 l
1 Gallon	128 fl.oz.	4 l

TEMPERATURES EQUIVALENTS

FAHRENHEIT (F)	CELSIUS (C) (APPROXIMATE)
225 °F	107 °C
250 °F	120 °C
275 °F	135 °C
300 °F	150 °C
325 °F	160 °C
350 °F	180 °C
375 °F	190 °C
400 °F	205 °C
425 °F	220 °C
450 °F	235 °C
475 °F	245 °C
500 °F	260 °C

Bonus

YOUR THOUGHTS MATTER!

Dear Valued Reader,

Expressing gratitude for joining us on this flavorful adventure. We trust the recipes have brought simplicity and flavor-packed wonders to your cooking experience.

YOUR FEEDBACK COUNTS

If this cookbook has infused culinary joy into your life, we invite you to share your insights by leaving a review on Amazon. Your reflections can guide prospective readers, serving as a compass for those seeking a delightful culinary journey.

Your support is truly invaluable!

HOW TO SHARE YOUR THOUGHTS:

- Visit the book's Amazon page.
- Navigate to the "Customer Reviews" section.
- Select "Write a Customer Review."
- Remember, your words carry weight!

YOUR BONUS AWAITS!

As a token of our appreciation, we're thrilled to offer you an exclusive bonus. Simply use your smartphone to scan the QR code below, and a special bonus will be delivered directly to your email.

HOW TO REDEEM YOUR BONUS:

- Activate your smartphone camera.
- Align it with the QR code.
- Once scanned, follow the on-screen instructions to claim your bonus.

Thank you once more for being an integral part of the Mediterranean Diet community. May these recipes continue to bring joy and flavor to your culinary endeavors.

Happy Cooking!

Warm Regards,
Olivia Davis

Made in the USA
Las Vegas, NV
10 May 2024

89724511R10052